NetResearch:

Finding Information Online

NetResearch:
Finding
Information
Online

Daniel J. Barrett

NetResearch: Finding Information Online
First Edition
by Daniel J. Barrett

Published by Songline Studios, Inc. and O'Reilly & Associates, Inc.
101 Morris Street, Sebastopol, CA 95472

Editor: Linda Lamb

Series Editor: Melissa Koch

Printing History: February 1997:   First Edition

Songline Guides is a trademark of Songline Studios, Inc.

Many of the designations used by manufacturers and sellers to distinguish their products are claimed as trademarks. Where those designations appear in this book, and Songline Studios, Inc., was aware of a trademark claim, the designations have been printed in caps or initial caps.

 This book is printed on acid-free paper with 85% recycled content, 15% post-consumer waste. The publishers are committed to using paper with the highest recycled content available consistent with high quality.

ISBN: 1-56592-245-X

Cover Design: Edie Freeman   [9/97]
Production Services: Thomas E. Dorsaneo

Contents

About the Author vii
Acknowledgments ix
Preface xi

Chapter 1 — Instant Gratification…and Beyond 1
Searching the Internet can be fruitful or frustrating. We provide some
reasons why it's sometimes hard to locate things online, introduce some "rules
for the road" for successful searching, and discuss the accuracy of information
found online.

Chapter 2 — Internet Basics 9
We present a basic overview of the World Wide Web, Usenet news,
electronic mail, and several other means of communication on the Internet.
For beginners only.

Chapter 3 — Views of the Internet 21
The Internet can be viewed in many ways, such as a library, a collection of resources, or a bunch of programs. Each view can help you search effectively
online, and we discuss their pros and cons. We also discuss the structure of
the Internet, explain how knowledge of computer names can speed up your
search, list some useful types of programs for searching, introduce searching
by keyword, and give a brief introduction to URLs.

Chapter 4 — Choosing an Effective Starting Point 37
The success and speed of a search depend on where you begin.
We discuss the advantages and disadvantages of various starting points:
Web search engines, specialized Web sites, Frequently Asked Questions
(FAQ) documents, public discussion groups, and your own intuition.

Chapter 5 — Web Searching Techniques 49
The World Wide Web is the premier method for locating information online.
We take an in-depth look at search engines, simple queries, and advanced
queries. Then we explain and compare numerous search strategies that work
with most search engines: specific search, general search, incremental search,
substring search, search-and-jump, and more.

Chapter 6 — Finding Places 75

A little knowledge of computer names and domains can help you locate Web
pages, FTP sites, and other Internet resources without doing any searching.
After discussing the basics of computer and domain naming on the Net, we
show you how to make intelligent guesses about the location of information.

Chapter 7 — Finding People 91

The Internet is great for tracking down colleagues, business partners, and
long-lost friends. We discuss how to locate people via email address databases, telephone databases, Usenet, the Web, and more.

Chapter 8 — Finding Kindred Spirits 107

No matter what interests you have, you can find an online community who
shares them. We discuss and compare three types of online meeting places:
mailing lists, public discussion groups, and chat groups, and how they are
best used.

Chapter 9 — Finding Freely Distributable Software 119

The Internet contains tons of free software for every type of computer.
We explain how to locate software by name, type, computer platform,
author's name, and filename, using tools such as Web search, Archie, and FTP.

Chapter 10 — Finding Information Again 133

The Internet is constantly changing. We discuss how to refind your favorite
resources quickly if they move or vanish, without much (or any) searching.
We also introduce bookmarks and bookmark management, discuss tips to
prevent bookmarks from becoming out of date, and cover basic Web page
creation for going beyond bookmarks.

Chapter 11 — Putting Information Online 151

By making a contribution to the Internet, you can help it grow and improve.
Volunteering can be profitable, educational, satisfying, and a great way to
make contacts. We discuss how to write effective FAQs, create mailing lists,
build Web resources, and create and moderate discussion groups.

Great Places to Start a Search 165
Answers to Quiz Questions 173
Index 181

About the Author

Dan Barrett attempted his first search on the Internet in 1985, when he typed "ftp *.*" and received an indecipherable error message. Since then, things have improved a bit (thank goodness), and Dan has worked as a UNIX system administrator, university instructor, software engineer, industry consultant, and Usenet newsgroup moderator. Currently, he is working on a Ph.D. in computer science at the University of Massachusetts.

Dan is the author of *Bandits on the Information Superhighway,* also from O'Reilly & Associates, and has published dozens of articles in popular computer and music magazines. His monthly column, "Net Smarts," appears in *Keyboard Magazine.*

When he's not navigating the Net, Dan likes to compose and record progressive rock music, play competitive volleyball, and cook. He and his wife, Lisa, reside in Boston.

Write to Dan on the Internet at *dbarrett@ora.com.*

Acknowledgments

As always, I thank my wonderful editor, Linda Lamb, for providing a perfect balance between editorial structure and writer's freedom. Whenever I get stuck, she's there with fresh ideas and inspiration. What more could one want? Linda's assistant, Carol Sholes, was also instrumental in keeping things running smoothly.

I extend huge thanks to this book's advisory panel for sharing their expertise and providing helpful advice and anecdotes throughout the book. They include Kathleen Callaway, technical writer at ILOG, a multinational producer of C++ programming tools; Ellie Cutler, Web services manager at O'Reilly & Associates; Fern Dickman, system manager at the General Clinical Research Centers of the Johns Hopkins University; Harv Laser, sysop of the Amiga Zone on CalWeb Internet Services, Web page developer, and journalist on personal computer topics; and Robert Strandh, professor of computer science at the University of Bordeaux, France. Several other people also contributed timely pieces of information, and I thank them: Kelly Madole (information about genealogy pages), Carol Sholes (the misspelled "recepe" example), Jason Tibbitts (GNUS tips), and Aaron Weiss (using a copy of Yahoo as one's home page).

Our technical review team did a terrific job locating trouble spots and suggesting improvements in preliminary versions of this manuscript: Mike King, Melissa Koch, Bob Parker, Michael Rosencrantz, Carol Sholes, Dave Sims, Larry Warner, and Aaron Weiss. Bob and Michael also contributed quotes within the text. Thanks folks!

I thank my parents, Drs. Judith and Stephen Barrett, for their love, encouragement, and many title suggestions; and my brother Ben and sister Debbie for their love and belief in me.

Finally, I thank Lisa: my wife, my partner, my closest friend, and without a doubt, the best thing I ever found on the Net.

Preface

THIS BOOK TEACHES RAPID, EFFECTIVE SEARCH TECHNIQUES

"I found it on the Internet." We hear this phrase increasingly often, and that's not surprising. Businesses and individuals have flocked to the Net, and new online information resources appear daily. Nowadays, if you have a question on virtually any topic, the answer is likely to be found somewhere on the Internet. Yes…somewhere.

But the Internet is a big place, and most people don't have time to keep track of the latest developments or the coolest new Web pages. When you need information online, sometimes you have to search for it. The rise of Web search engines, like Yahoo and Lycos, have made this process easier; but not everything is located on the Web, and search engines aren't always the fastest way to find things. In addition, there are usually several ways to reach the same place online, and some routes are significantly shorter than others. So when you're logged in and need an answer *right now,* where should you look? Perhaps more importantly, *how* should you look?

Whether you use the Internet for business or recreation, there's no need to waste time or money (online fees) searching inefficiently. The more quickly you can find the best information, the more productive you'll be. That's what this book is all about.

YOU'LL LEARN A LASTING SKILL

Many of today's "introduction to the Internet" books discuss Net searching, particularly on the World Wide Web, in a strange way. Like cookbooks, they provide step-by-step instructions for locating particular Web pages. Some books, in fact, are just big lists of Web sites: so-called Yellow Pages of the Internet. The problem with this approach is that the Internet changes rapidly. A year later, or even by the time the book goes to press, many Web pages have moved or disappeared, and the book becomes out of date—about as useful as an old telephone directory.

This book, however, is built to last. It's not just a big list of Web pages (though we do include one as an appendix to help you get started). Instead, it teaches general strategies and *search techniques* that will continue to work even while the Net changes around us. Can't find one of the Web pages listed in another book? No problem. We'll show you where (and how) to look next.

In short, *this is how the experts do it.* Not by memorizing lists that go out of date, but by developing intuition.

THIS BOOK HAS FOUR PARTS

Chapters 1–4 introduce searching on the Internet. They answer the questions: What is searching? How is the Internet organized? Where do I begin my search? People already familiar with the Web, email, Usenet, and FTP may skip Chapter 2, but all readers should at least look over Chapters 1, 3 and 4 , even if they have already done a fair amount of searching on the Net.

Chapters 5–9 are the meat of the book, describing dozens of methods for power searching on the Net. These chapters are intended not only to teach particular techniques, but also to help you think like a searcher. Each chapter focuses on finding a different kind of practical information.

Chapters 10 and 11 discuss topics related to searching: how to remember where items are located on the Net, how to find them when they move, and how to contribute your own.

The book concludes with a list of Internet resources to assist your searches on the Net. In addition, each chapter includes pointers to related resources.

WE ASSUME SOME THINGS ABOUT THE READER

To make the best use of this book, you need a computer account with access to the Internet. Your account could be with a commercial on-line service provider, with a PPP or SLIP provider, or on a computer directly connected to the Internet. At the very least, your account *must* allow you to send and receive electronic mail over the Internet and browse the World Wide Web. If your account also gives you access to Usenet and allows you to transfer files with FTP, this is ideal.

This book includes special tips for users of America Online (version 3.0), CompuServe (version 3.0.1), Microsoft Network (MSN Program Viewer version 2.00.52), Prodigy (version 1.5b), and direct connections via Windows, Macintosh, and UNIX.

YOU CAN MEASURE YOUR PROGRESS

Every chapter ends with a quiz to test your mastery of the material. For instance, you'll be challenged to locate information on a particular topic or to discover somebody's electronic mail address. Some questions will have one right answer, but others will have several depending on how you search.

As you take each quiz, you should have two goals. The first, more obvious goal is to find the requested information and get that glowing feeling of satisfaction for a job well done. The second and perhaps more important goal is to notice *how* you find the information. Sometimes you'll be asked to find the same thing in two different ways, say, once with a Web search engine and once by making an educated guess. For these questions, your method is even more important than getting the right answer, because you'll be able to use this method over and over to find new information in the future.

So try the quizzes. We've tried to make them both practical and entertaining. And if you enjoy a bit of competition, see how quickly an officemate or friend can locate the same information online. Then compare strategies.

Instant Gratification... and Beyond

The Internet is one of the world's largest sources of publicly available information. Thanks to the growth of the World Wide Web, millions of electronic resources around the globe are at our fingertips. To help us deal with this incredible amount of data, a new skill has arisen: *Internet searching*. Given any topic—mutual funds, plane schedules, beer, harpsichords, or whatever—anyone with an Internet-capable computer account can search the Net for information on that topic.

Searching, however, is not the same thing as finding. The Internet is a jumble of facts, opinions, stories, conversations, arguments, artwork, mistakes, trivia, and one-of-a-kind knowledge. There's little organization or consistency. And yet, it's possible to navigate the Net effectively and reap great rewards.

This chapter provides a quick introduction to Internet searching, both its benefits and its difficulties.

- Introduction to searching.
- Why searches may fail.
- The art of searching.
- Accuracy isn't guaranteed online.

YOU CAN SEARCH THE INTERNET

Assuming you have an Internet-capable computer account, let's jump-start this book with a quick example. (If you don't have an account yet, just follow along.)

Run your Web browser (see the sidebar "Connecting to the Web" if you need help with this) and connect to Yahoo, a popular site on the Internet. Yahoo is a special kind of Web site called a *search engine*. If you type a few words onto the Web page, Yahoo attempts to locate other Web pages related to your words.

We'll connect to Yahoo by providing its Web address—called its *URL* (Uniform Resource Locator)—to the browser. This is generally accomplished using the browser's Open, Open URL, or Open Location command. When prompted for a URL, type:

http://www.yahoo.com

If all goes well, you'll soon see Yahoo's main Web page, which at press time looks like Figure 1-1.

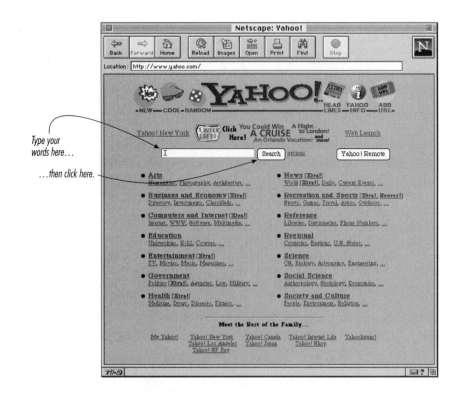

FIGURE 1-1
Yahoo's main Web page

Hmmm...what shall we search for? Let's look for information on one of the world's greatest searchers, Sherlock Holmes. In the space provided, type the words `Sherlock Holmes` and press the on-screen Search button.

In a moment, Yahoo should respond with dozens of "pointers" to further information about Sherlock Holmes: tributes, lists of stories, Holmes t-shirts, Holmes museums, the life of Sir Arthur Conan Doyle (his creator), and more. These pointers, called *links,* lead to other Web pages. To follow a link, select it with your mouse, and its associated Web page will appear, containing information and more links. You can then follow those links to still more Web pages, and so on, and so on. Follow some links and see where they take you.

Welcome to the World Wide Web. As you can see, it wasn't very hard to locate tons of information about Sherlock Holmes. There must be more to searching, however...or else this would be a very short book.

Connecting to the Web

This book assumes you already have a computer account with an online service provider that enables you to connect to the Internet. To get to the World Wide Web, connect to your provider and do the following:

- *America Online:* Enter the keyword web.
- *CompuServe:* GO INTERNET. Then select Enter An Internet Site.
- *Microsoft Network*: Connect to MSN and click the "Reveal Internet Toolbar" button. A box labeled Address will appear where you may type URLs..
- *Prodigy:* Enter the jumpword web.
- *Computer with PPP, SLIP, or direct TCP/IP connection*: If you do not already have a World Wide Web browser such as Netscape Navigator, Mosaic, or Microsoft Internet Explorer, you or your system administrator need to obtain and install one. Then run the browser like any other program.

UNFORTUNATELY, SOME SEARCHES FAIL

One reason our Sherlock Holmes search succeeded so easily is that our goal was very general. Any information on Sherlock Holmes was good enough. Suppose you had a more specific goal, the name of a Sherlock Holmes story you read a long time ago. All you remember is that the victims were killed by a poisonous snake. So you might try asking Yahoo to look for:

```
Sherlock Holmes and the poisonous snake
```

This time, unfortunately, Yahoo responds "No matching Yahoo sites." In other words, Yahoo didn't find anything that matches your goal. The search has failed.

Does this mean there's no information on the whole Internet about Sherlock Holmes and poisonous snakes? No, all it means is that Yahoo couldn't find what you requested. Maybe your request could be stated differently, for instance, by typing `poison` instead of `poisonous`. Or perhaps Yahoo is the wrong place to look. (Incidentally, the Sherlock Holmes story mentioned is *The Adventure of the Speckled Band*.)

Searches can fail for other reasons too. Suppose you need to know the definition of a word, so you decide to find a dictionary on the Net. You tell Yahoo to look for `dictionary`. In return, you get hundreds of links: a Japanese-Danish dictionary, a dictionary of famous quotations, the "Devil's Dictionary" by Ambrose Bierce, a genealogy dictionary, an English-Romanian dictionary of proverbs, a rhyming dictionary, a nutrient dictionary from a vitamin manufacturer, a dictionary of railway terminology...! There might be a traditional dictionary buried in this pile of data, but who has time to look? Sometimes, too much information is just as bad as too little.

In general, a variety of problems can occur while searching on the Net:

- You could search for a long time but find nothing. It's possible that the information isn't available on the Internet, but it's also possible that you aren't looking in the right place or asking in the best way.
- You could find so much information that you can't possibly weed through it to find what you need. (A simple search can easily locate more than 100,000 vaguely relevant Web pages.)
- You could encounter a slow network connection...at a time when you need answers quickly.
- The computer that holds the information you need could be down for repairs.
- You could find what you need, take note of the location, but later discover that it has vanished. (The Net changes rapidly.)

In other words, searching can sometimes be quite a challenge. Despite what media pundits may say about the information treasures of the Internet, some work may be required to locate what you need online.

This book is designed to teach you to be an effective Internet navigator, seeking out information, locating it rapidly, and avoiding pitfalls.

SEARCHING THE INTERNET IS AN ART

Do you know somebody—perhaps a friend or coworker—who always finds great stuff online? Have you ever wondered how he or she does it? Chances are, the answer is a combination of experience, insight, and perseverance. (And probably a little luck.) It takes a certain outlook to become a successful Net searcher, and throughout this book, you'll find some important themes that reflect this attitude. I call these themes the *Internet Searcher's Rules for the Road*.

- *Carefully choose a starting place.* As the old saying says, sometimes "you can't get there from here." Different starting points may lead to different results.

- *Don't assume failure too quickly.* When a search program responds "nothing found," don't give up. Try a few variations on your search. If these don't produce results either, try other starting places, programs, and search techniques.

- *Don't assume success too quickly.* Even when you locate what you need, there might be another source of information available that is better. Don't be too loyal to one Web site or one search technique. Keep an open mind. Experiment.

- *Think about your route.* Even if you reached your goal, there might have been a faster way to get there. Pay attention when a search strategy provides quick results: the same strategy might be usable in other situations.

- *Know your tools.* Read the manual. Use the online help. Try out all the commands and options. Make sure your search software is the latest version, or at least a recent one.

- *Intuition is your best search tool.* The Internet changes rapidly, and so does the software we use to access it. Knowledge, on the other hand, accumulates. As you learn from experience, you'll get progressively better at tackling new situations.

Net experts use these principles to locate what they need in the ever-changing online world. And when you've finished this book, so will you.

ACCURACY ISN'T GUARANTEED ONLINE

The Net can be a terrific source of information…or misinformation. Just because something appears on a Web page doesn't make it true. Material on the Internet is written by thousands of individuals with differing opinions, motivations, and levels of expertise. Since much of the material has not gone through any editorial process, you're bound to encounter errors, omissions, and biases online…even lies.

How can you tell if an online resource is believable? This is a difficult task, similar to judging material you receive by postal mail, read in the back of magazines, or see on television "infomercials." Your best bet is to identify the source of the information, though this may be difficult. Your experience with the source will then determine how much trust you have in that information.

The URL (address) of a Web page can provide some assurance that its information is legitimate. If the Web page resides on a computer belonging to a relevant, official organization, this is a good sign. For example, a table of postal mail rates is likely to be accurate if found on *www.usps.gov*, the Web site for the United States Postal Service. (Chapter 6 will explain how to examine a URL and identify the computer containing the Web page, and from there, the sponsoring organization.) Web sites for major newspapers and magazines have the same credibility as their in-print counterparts, and well-known companies generally try to keep their Web sites accurate, though they may still use advertising hype. On the other hand, an advertisement for unproven health products, on a Web site you've never heard of before, that asks you to send money to a post office box, should be treated with extreme skepticism.

Some of the major issues of accuracy online are:

- *Mistakes.* Typographical errors, factual errors, accidental omissions, incorrect URLs, careless statements, and ambiguity can occur in any material online. If you discover any of the above, be sure to inform the author or the maintainer of the material. Usually their email address is found near the information: on the same Web page, on the main page of the Web site, in the headers of a

Usenet article, or in the return address of an email message. Some Web sites even have fill-in-the-blanks forms for reporting errors.

- *Outdated information.* Material online is not always kept up to date. When events happen in the world, Web page creators may be slow, forget, or neglect to update their pages correspondingly. Updated information may become available online in a different location from the original, with no indication that this is so. In addition, articles written years ago still float around the Net, sometimes with the date of authorship missing, so it's not easy to tell the material is old. Even Web page links become obsolete as locations change.

  There's no easy way to ensure that the material you find is up to date, other than contacting the author or maintainer and asking. (As with errors and omissions, notify the author or maintainer if you find outdated information.)

- *Opinions stated as facts.* Some kinds of online information are obviously opinions, such as product reviews and political beliefs. Other opinions can easily be dressed up to look like facts. Consider investment advice, for example. A Web site may contain factual charts and graphs illustrating the rise and fall of the stock market, but if it states that a particular stock will go up in the future, this is speculation and therefore opinion.

  In general, most of what you'll read on the Net will be opinions, so remember the old rule *caveat emptor* ("buyer beware"). Anybody can say just about anything they want online, and it's up to you to judge the validity of the source.

- *Bias and conflict of interest.* When examining information online, consider the source. For example, suppose you encounter a Web page comparing the long-distance rates of AT&T, MCI, and Sprint. You might treat this page with differing levels of skepticism depending on its source. If the page appeared on *Consumer Reports* magazine's Web site, you might view the comparison with high confidence. If it appeared on the Web site of (say) AT&T, or of a fourth long-distance company who claimed its rates were lower than those compared, you might be more concerned about bias. If you found the comparison on a random user's home page, you might not know what to think.

  Paid sponsorship is also an important factor in judging material. Some Web sites pretend to provide unbiased recommendations of products or services, when really they recommend anybody who pays them a fee. For example, suppose you encounter a Web page that recommends attorneys in your geographic area. Does it list all the attorneys, or only those who have paid to be listed? As another example, suppose you locate a Web page about abortion. You might view it differently if it's sponsored by the Christian Coalition as opposed to Planned Parenthood.

- *Fraud.* Although most people on the Internet behave honestly, there are always troublemakers in any crowd. Be aware that phony businesses, illegal money-making schemes, deceptive advertisements, and hoaxes are sometimes found online. The Web lets anybody put flashy, promotional literature onto the Net at very low cost, so don't be misled by the look of a Web page. Be skeptical of claims that seem too good to be true.

Nevertheless, the Net remains a great resource on countless topics. Don't be put off by this cautionary information. You just have to take some online "facts" with a grain of salt.

QUIZ: Instant gratification... and beyond

1. Connect to Yahoo and perform searches for the following topics:

   (a) Sherlock Holmes

   (b) dictionary

   (c) The name of your favorite musical artist

   (d) The name of your favorite sports team

   (e) The name of a company whose product you recently purchased

   (f) Your own name

   What happened? Did you get satisfactory results?

2. Repeat the previous searches, but this time do your searching at InfoSeek:

   http://www.infoseek.com

   Were the results more or less useful than Yahoo's? (Note: Don't make any grand judgments about Yahoo vs. InfoSeek yet. Each has advantages over the other.)

3. Connect to the Web page:

   http://www.ora.com/catalog/netresearch/

   where you'll find a page specially devoted to this book. I'll be keeping it updated with new and exciting stuff related to searching on the Internet.

4. Spend another hour messing around with Web search engines. Have fun.

Internet Basics

2

This chapter provides a quick overview of some major forms of communication on the Net.

- *The World Wide Web,* a multimedia information source organized into convenient "pages" for browsing. (We'll also mention *Gopher* and *FTP,* two predecessors of the Web.)
- *Usenet news,* a worldwide set of public discussion groups.
- *Electronic mail,* for sending messages directly to another user.
- *Local resources* available from your online service provider. Typically, these resources are available only to members.

These are not the only ways of communicating on the Net, but they're the main ones used in this book.

This chapter is intended for beginners. If you're already familiar with the topics above, skip to Chapter 3.

THE WEB CONNECTS INFORMATION RESOURCES

World Wide Web FAQ

http://www.boutell.com/faq/

For answers to common questions about the World Wide Web, check out this site.

The *World Wide Web* (sometimes called "WWW" or "the Web") is a way of communicating words, pictures, and sound on the Internet. Information on the Web is organized into "pages," called *Web pages,* that are much like the pages of a magazine. Figure 2-1 illustrates a typical Web page.

Using a Web-browsing program (or "browser") like Netscape Navigator or Microsoft Internet Explorer, you can navigate from Web page to Web page using a convenient, point-and-click user interface. For example, suppose you are reading a Web page about baseball. Click on the name of your favorite team, and a new Web page appears, displaying the team's current players. Click on a player's name, and a new Web page appears, displaying the player's photograph and

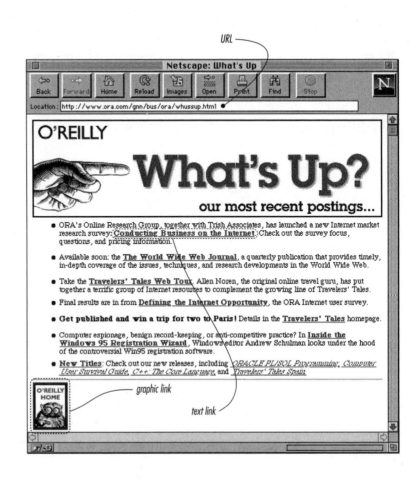

FIGURE 2-1

A typical Web page

batting average. Click on the photo, and a spoken message from the player is heard through your computer speakers.

A *link* is a word or picture you select on a Web page, usually by clicking your mouse on it, leading you to a new page. Web pages and their links are usually organized logically, as in our baseball example, but they don't have to be. If somebody wants to make a silly Web page combining baseball, Barbie dolls, and brain surgery, this is perfectly OK.

Web pages are created by interested users and organizations around the world. A Web page you view might be stored on your local computer, or it might come from another computer far away. The beauty of the Web is that you aren't required to know where the pages are kept. Just select a link, and the associated Web page will pop up on your screen, even if it has to be transmitted from a computer you've never heard of on the other side of the globe. Depending on who your online service provider is, you might be able to create your own Web pages as well, complete with links to other pages.

■ I can get decent technical information without having to wait on hold forever. —Fern Dickman ■ The opinion of common people, not published through an editorial filter. Of course you have to take everything with a grain of salt, but what you hear is so much more detailed and real than on the news. —Ellie Cutler	**What do you like about the Web?**

EACH WEB PAGE HAS A URL

Every Web page has a unique name, called a *Uniform Resource Locator*, or *URL* (pronounced "U–R–L"), so it can be located. Often this locating is done automatically when you select a link, but you can also jump to a Web page directly using its URL, as we did with Yahoo in Chapter 1. URLs can look pretty cryptic. For example, here is the URL that leads to the main Web page of O'Reilly & Associates:

http://www.ora.com

For now, you don't need to understand the language of URLs. Just think of them like the Dewey Decimal System of the Internet. In a library, we don't need to understand the meaning of each Dewey Decimal number (for instance, that B972.41Q means "hyena dentistry"), but we do need to know how to locate a book given its Dewey Decimal number. Likewise, we don't have to care that *http://www.afws.org/ main/* is the home page of the Albanian Flamingo-Watching Society, but we do need to know how to tell a Web browser to connect to a page, given its URL. Your browser likely has an Open URL command to let you type a URL. Table 2-1 shows the commands for common browsers.

To be an effective Internet searcher, you do need to be comfortable with URLs. It's possible for a person to browse the Web for years and never bother with URLs, but when the searching gets tough, a little URL knowledge can keep you going. You don't have to be the Grand URL Wizard of All Time and Space, but it doesn't hurt to take a few lessons. We'll discuss URLs further in Chapter 3.

Browser	Command
America Online browser	No command needed: just type the URL in the space provided. Alternatively, select **Keyword** from the main AOL menu.
CompuServe 3.0	No command needed: just type the URL in the Page box.
CompuServe Mosaic	**Open** or **Open Location** from the browser.
Lynx	Type the letter g.
Microsoft Internet Explorer	**Open** or **Open Location** from the browser.
Microsoft Network	Click on the "Reveal Internet Toolbar" button. In the space provided, labeled Address, type the URL.
NCSA Mosaic	**Open** from the browser.
Netscape Navigator	**Open** or **Open Location** from the browser.
Prodigy Web Browser	**Get URL** from the browser.

TABLE 2-1:
Connecting to a URL

URL (begins with gopher://)

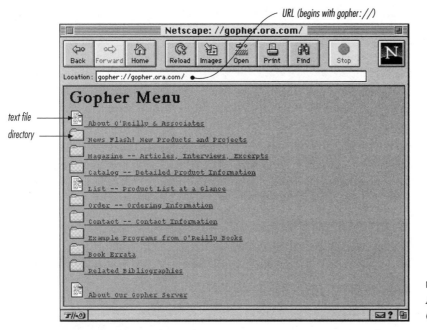

text file

directory

FIGURE 2-2
*A typical
Gopher display*

GOPHER SITES DISPLAY ONLY TEXT

Another information source similar to the World Wide Web is *Gopher*. Gopher is much more limited, however. It uses only text and can link only to other Gopher pages, whereas the Web has pictures and sound and can link to many types of pages. If you connect to a Gopher site using a Web browser, you'll see a fairly barren-looking menu of choices, as in Figure 2-2.

Gopher was developed before the Web came into existence and is still used here and there, but the Web has mostly replaced it. Web browsing programs can access Gopher data, so you don't need to learn a separate Gopher program.

Gopher Jewels
http://galaxy.einet.net/GJ/
This site contains an interesting set of Gopher sites.

FTP LETS YOU TRANSFER FILES BETWEEN COMPUTERS

File Transfer Protocol, or *FTP*, is an old, commonly used method for sending files from one Internet computer to another. Computers that make files available by FTP are called *FTP sites*. FTP sites are generally used for uploading and downloading freely distributable files,

FTP FAQ
*http://ftp.wustl.edu/
~aminet/ftpfaq*
Further details on FTP are available from this site.

such as freeware and shareware programs. Throughout the book, we'll mention FTP sites where interesting files can be found.

Originally, FTP required users to type commands like "get" and "put" to download and upload files, but most new FTP programs have point-and-click graphical interfaces. Web browsers too can download files using FTP. They present files as links, as in Figure 2-3.

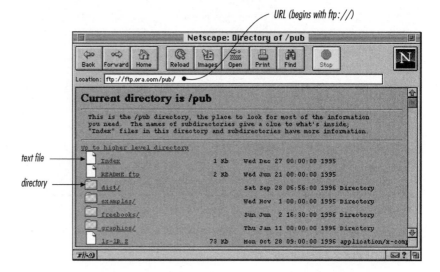

FIGURE 2-3
A typical FTP site

To download a file, just click on its link.

Even though FTP sites can be accessed via the Web, there are sometimes advantages to using a standalone FTP program instead of a Web browser, as we'll see in Chapter 9.

Usenet Info Center
http://sunsite.unc.edu/usenet-i/

This site can serve as an introduction to Usenet.

USENET NEWS IS A SET OF PUBLIC DISCUSSION GROUPS

So far, we've looked at communication methods that are relatively solitary. You can browse Web pages, Gopher menus, and FTP sites without interacting with other people. Sometimes, however, you'd like to have a discussion with interested people on the Net, sharing opinions, trading expertise, or engaging in debate. This is what *Usenet* is all about. Usenet is a collection of computers worldwide that allows people to hold convenient, public discussions. These discussions are called *Usenet news*. Not all computers on the Internet are part of Usenet, but many are. Usenet is sometimes called News, NetNews or Internet Newsgroups.

Usenet news comprises thousands of discussion groups, called *newsgroups*. Each newsgroup has a specific topic. Whether you want to talk about chemistry, alternative music, feminism, or your favorite television show, there's a newsgroup for you. Using a computer program called a *newsreader,* you can subscribe to newsgroups, read the articles, and write your own articles. Contributing your own article is called *posting,* and the articles themselves are sometimes called *posts.* When you post an article, copies are transmitted throughout Usenet for other people to read.

Most Web browsers can access Usenet news via a special kind of URL. Often, the browser will display articles in a separate window specially designed for news reading.

Newsgroup names indicate their topics. The names look like a bunch of words separated by dots (periods). For example, *rec.arts.movies. reviews* is the newsgroup devoted to movie reviews. As you read a newsgroup name from left to right, the topic becomes more specific. In the name *rec.arts.movies.reviews,* for example, the leftmost word, *rec,* indicates that the topic is a recreation. The next word, *arts,* indicates that the recreation is an art. The third word, *movies,* indicates that the art is movies, and the last word, *reviews,* indicates that movies are reviewed in this newsgroup. See Figure 2-4 for a typical article from *rec.arts.movies.reviews.*

Many online service providers have local services similar to Usenet, typically called "message boards," "forums," or "discussion groups," available to their members. Usenet is open to all users, however (assuming your online service provider supports it), with more than 18,000 newsgroups and millions of participants worldwide. (Most computers don't carry every newsgroup, though.)

```
newsgroup ———   Newsgroups: rec.arts.movies.reviews
poster's name ——  From: em@arts.harnwell.no (Emma Luplet)
subject ———     Subject: REVIEW: The Beagle and the Buzzard
                Date: Fri Jun 07 11:31:16 EDT 1996
                Organization: Harnwell Art Industries, Norway
header ———      Lines: 206

body text ———         Rarely does a motion picture touch the senses like
                Marv Ostrich's latest film, "The Beagle and the Buzzard,"
                which opened today to record-breaking crowds in Oslo.
                Starring relative unknowns and filmed on a shoestring
                budget, "Beagle" nevertheless rivals any of this year's
                big-budget films and their mega-stars. Perhaps the most
```

FIGURE 2-4
A typical Usenet article

USENET NEWS IS ALSO A SEARCHABLE SOURCE

Usenet began life as a set of discussion groups. Articles expired and were deleted after a few days, so nobody thought of Usenet as a permanent information archive. In recent years, however, organizations have begun storing Usenet news in searchable databases. With a few mouse clicks, you can now locate articles written by particular people, about particular subjects, or containing particular words. We'll discuss these Usenet search engines in Chapter 4.

In this book, we'll view Usenet both as a set of discussion groups and a stored information source. Each view is useful for a different kind of searching, as we shall see.

What do you like about Usenet?

- With tens of thousands of newsgroups, every subject you can think of is covered. An amazing number of people use Usenet and you can ask just about anything and get a reply. Often tens or hundreds of replies. It's also a great way to buy and sell personal items. —Harv Laser

- You hear from people who aren't professional writers, so their information won't show up anywhere else. Certainly not in the traditional media. —Ellie Cutler

- Access to experts in nearly every discipline—people with a wealth of knowledge and experience who are willing to share it. —Bob Parker

- There are so many participants, and you often get several different points of view on an issue. —Robert Strandh

EMAIL IS FOR SENDING MESSAGES DIRECTLY TO OTHER USERS

Electronic mail, or *email*, is the most common way that users communicate on the Internet. It works a lot like ordinary postal mail, except that email is much faster. On a good day, an email message can reach a user halfway around the world in a matter of seconds.

Email is like a cross between postal mail and a telephone call. Using an *email program*, you compose a message that you want to send to another user. You also specify who should receive the message, by giving the recipient's *email address*. Finally, you use the email program's Send command, and the message is sent rapidly across

sender ——————
recipient ——————
subject ——————

```
From:  laf@mail.bc.edu (Leon Feldburg, Ph.D.)
To:  djb@redwood.com (Denny Baron)
Subject:  Re:  Possible academic/industry collaboration?
Date:  Tue, 28 May 1996 11:00:30 - 0400
```

body text ——————

```
Hi Denny - thanks for your note. I think you're
right: we do have a mutual interest, and I think
a lot of good could come of a collaborative effort.
Could you discuss this over coffee tomorrow? I'll
buy.

-L
```

FIGURE 2-5
A typical email message

computer cables and phone lines to its intended recipient. The message is then stored in the recipient's *electronic mailbox*, a file on the recipient's computer. The recipient can then read the mail at his or her leisure.

Most users on the Internet have an email address for receiving email. An email address usually looks like a username, followed by an "at" symbol (@), followed by the name of a computer. For example, the user *frieda* with an account on the machine *cs.berkeley.edu* has the email address *frieda@cs.berkeley.edu*.

When other users send you email, you can read it with an email program. See Figure 2-5 for a typical email message.

Email programs also let you reply to messages, save them, print them, delete them, or forward them to other users.

People don't often think about email as a tool for searching the Internet, but occasionally it's quite effective. Some individuals and organizations set up *auto-responding* email addresses for distributing information. If you send an email message to one of these addresses, a computer program, called an *auto-responder*, automatically replies with the information you want. Email is also the basis for Internet mailing lists, discussed in Chapter 8.

THINGS CHANGE ON THE NET

Web URLs, Gopher sites, FTP sites, Usenet newsgroups, email addresses, and other "addresses" on the Net are subject to change without notice. If a Web page (or other resource) listed in this book seems to have disappeared, don't worry. The search techniques we'll cover should help you find the new location of the page if it has moved, or to find other, similar pages on the Web.

"The History of the Internet" can be found on PBS's Web site: *http://www.pbs.org/ internet/history*

"EFF's (Extended) Guide to the Internet"

http://www.eff.org/papers/eegtti

See this site for an overview of the Internet and its resources.

COMMERCIAL ONLINE SERVICE PROVIDERS HAVE RESOURCES

The resources we've discussed so far are widely available on the Internet. Commercial online service providers often have additional, local resources available only to their members. Here's how to find out what's available from some of the major providers, while you are logged on as a member.

- *America Online*: Use the Find command to locate local information. The `services` keyword is another way to search for local AOL services. Finally, the `keyword` keyword displays a list of all available services.

- *CompuServe*: The CompuServe Directory, available from CompuServe's Access or Help menu, summarizes all of CompuServe's available services using a point-and-click interface. Alternatively, use `GO QUICK` or `GO INDEX` for a list of available services.

- *Microsoft Network*: The Find menu offers several ways to search MSN by keyword or by subject.

- *Prodigy*: Use the Search menu to search for local services. Alternatively, use the jumpword `A-Z Index` for a list of all available services.

TOOLS ARE JUST THE BEGINNING

Once you have learned to use a Web browser, email program, or other Internet-related programs, you're ready to start roaming around the Net. If you want to be an effective Internet searcher, however, knowledge of programs is not enough. That's why this book is different from others that focus on every tiny detail of these programs. Instead, we'll focus on general *strategies* for locating anything you want on the Net, and all you'll need to know are the most basic features of your programs. Even when the tools change (and they will), these search strategies will still work for you.

QUIZ: Internet basics

1. Find out what kind of software your online service provider supplies for browsing the Web, reading Usenet news, using FTP, and using electronic mail.

2. Connect to the Web site of O'Reilly & Associates:

   http://www.ora.com

   to see what it's like to visit a Web site. Browse around and see what you find.

3. Connect to the Gopher site of O'Reilly & Associates:

   gopher://gopher.ora.com

   to see what it's like to visit a Gopher site. Browse around and see what you find.

4. Connect to the FTP site:

   ftp://gatekeeper.dec.com

   so you can see what it's like to use an FTP site. Select the link README.ftp for information about this site. Browse around and see what else you can find.

5. If your online service provider receives Usenet news and supplies a newsreader, use it to read the newsgroup *news.announce.newusers*. This newsgroup contains introductory information for new users of Usenet.

6. Use your Web browser to connect to the newsgroup *news.announce.newusers* via the URL:

   news:news.announce.newusers

7. Say hello to me, Dan Barrett, by sending an email message to *dbarrett@ora.com*.

Views of the Internet 3

There are a number of possible views of the Internet. For example:

- It's a gigantic bunch of *computers*.
- It's a collection of *programs*.
- It's a collection of online *resources*.
- It's like a worldwide electronic *library*.

Before we start discussing power search techniques, it's important to know how to *think* about searching. The goal of this chapter is to get you comfortable viewing the Internet in multiple ways. With practice, you'll get a feel for which views are best under different circumstances.

DIVERSE VIEWS
ARE USEFUL

If you ask several people to describe the Internet, you'll receive a variety of answers. One person might think of it as a gigantic bunch of *computers* connected to one another. Someone else may see it as a collection of *programs,* like email software and World Wide Web browsers, that help us communicate and find things. Yet another person could tell us the Internet is a collection of online *resources,* like Web sites, newsgroups, and mailing lists, each of which is designed around a topic or theme. A fourth person might say it's like a worldwide electronic *library,* where you can look up information on various topics.

Each of these descriptions contains some truth. You see, there isn't just one correct way to view the Internet. There are many ways. Your view depends on how you use the Net: what you need to *do* online.

In this book, our goal is to locate information quickly on a variety of topics. So, which of these views is the most useful for us? The answer is: all of them! A key to effective searching is to be able to *change* your view of the Internet as needed. If you know exactly where to look and want to get there quickly, it's good to view the Net as a bunch of computers, so you can jump immediately to the computer of your choice. On the other hand, if you need information on a particular topic but have no idea where to find it, the library view is useful. Viewing the Internet as a collection of programs or resources has other advantages.

When people view the Internet in only one way, searching can be difficult. Some users, for example, view the Net only as a library, using a Web search engine as they would a card catalog. But what happens when the search engine says, "nothing found?" These people give up. The desired information might still be out there, but it can't be located by this method. What to do? Change viewpoint, and search in a different way.

THE INTERNET IS
LESS STRUCTURED
THAN IT LOOKS

If you spend time using Web search engines, the Internet may seem quite organized. Yahoo (*http://www.yahoo.com*), for example, groups its Web links into logical categories—Arts, Education, Entertainment, Government—and from there, into subcategories. This convenient ordering, however, is not truly how the Internet is organized. It's just the way Yahoo's administrators like to group things. In short, it's their view of the Net, and when you access Yahoo, you adopt this view to help you search.

The Internet isn't conveniently organized. It's too big, and it's constantly being modified by thousands of people who don't know each other. An organized view like Yahoo's imposes order on the chaos and provides a structure for your search. But it's not *the* structure. It's just *a* structure, and it may or may not serve your purposes. That's why it's important to know how, and when, to change your view.

VIEW 1:
THE INTERNET IS A
BUNCH OF COMPUTERS

In ancient times (say, the mid-1980s), people viewed the Internet largely as a collection of networked computers. To find information on a given topic, you needed to know which machine stored it. For free PC software, you connected to the computer *simtel20.arpa*. Mac users likewise downloaded from *sumex-aim.stanford.edu*, and Commodore users from *swan.ulowell.edu*. Movie reviews were on *ashpool.micro.umn.edu*. And so on. There was no rhyme or reason about which computers had which data. You just had to know.

major categories

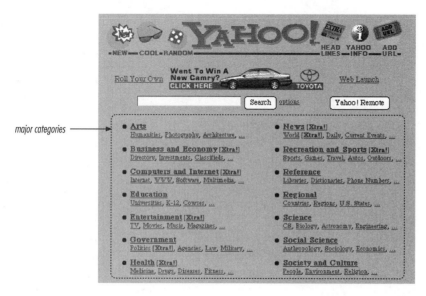

FIGURE 3-1
Yahoo's main page

This view of the Internet had an obvious disadvantage. To be an efficient searcher, one had to know lots of computer names. People devised shortcuts to avoid memorization. For instance, they posted gigantic catalogs on Usenet every month, listing which computers contained which information (a practice that continues to this day). But overall, things were hard to find.

KNOWING COMPUTER NAMES CAN SPEED UP YOUR SEARCH

Every Internet computer has a unique name. A computer name looks like a bunch of words separated by periods, like *compuserve.com* (CompuServe) or *www.math.harvard.edu* (the Web site of the math department at Harvard University). The words in a computer name have meanings, but we won't need to know the details until Chapter 6. For now, just be aware that computer names with the final word *com* belong to companies, and those ending in *edu* belong to educational institutions (colleges, universities). The next-to-last word generally tells you whose computer it is (CompuServe, Harvard).

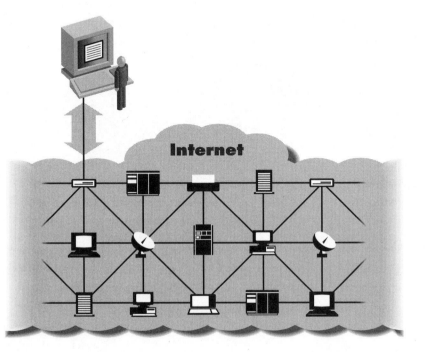

FIGURE 3-2

The Internet can be viewed as a collection of computers

If you know some computer names when you search the Net, you can gain an advantage: speed. For example, suppose you need technical information about Microsoft Windows. Instead of connecting to a Web search engine, typing "Microsoft," waiting for the result, selecting the result, and finally getting to Microsoft's Web site, you can zip directly to the desired computer. In this example, you could grab things quickly via the Web from *www.microsoft.com* or by FTP from *ftp.microsoft.com*.

This example assumes I somehow knew that Microsoft's computer names end with *microsoft.com*. This was not done by memorization, though. I figured it out by guessing. It wasn't a hard guess; after all, *microsoft.com* is perhaps the most natural name for Microsoft to use. But there is an art to guessing computer names and domain names intelligently. Chapter 6 discusses this subject.

Another reason to be aware of computer names is to figure out their physical locations. For example, *ftp.stanford.edu* is in California (Stanford University), and *ftp.funet.fi* is in Finland (*fi*). Suppose you need a freeware software package, and both of these computers have it. If you live on the west coast of the United States, which computer do you think you can access more quickly? Intuition says Stanford. If you can get your software from a closer computer, the download may take less time.

Distance isn't the only factor that makes a Net connection fast or slow; the computer's processor and network hardware also affect transfer speed. And geographic distance (miles) can have less effect than network distance (the cables and hardware that lie between two computers). In addition, some computers are busier than others, meaning they can't devote much time or energy to your requests. But geographic distance, especially internationally, can be a reasonable way to predict transfer speed. Someday, Internet communication might be so rapid that distance won't matter. For now, however, it can make a big difference.

VIEW 2: THE INTERNET IS A COLLECTION OF PROGRAMS

Some introductory books explain the Internet by teaching the reader how to use programs. According to these books, if you learn how to use a World Wide Web browser, a Usenet newsreader, an email program, and other software, then you'll be ready to find anything you want.

This view can be quite useful. If you're skilled at using a Web browser, for example, then you'll be able to navigate quickly from page to page, locating items of interest and saving their locations for later visits.

The downside of this view, however, is that it ignores intuition. Even if people learn every single feature of a Web browser, it doesn't make them effective searchers. You don't become a great piano player simply by learning how to press each note on the keyboard and how to work the pedals. Similarly, you don't become a great Net searcher by knowing a hundred commands.

LEARN A FEW PROGRAMS VERY WELL

Still, there is no substitute for practice. If you know your software well, you won't waste time hunting through manuals and asking questions of your system staff. You should have at least the following tools under your belt.

- *An email program.* You probably use one already, but how well do you know its capabilities? Learn the different options for sending, receiving, and (especially) organizing your mail.

- *A Web browser.* Find out what all of the buttons and menu items do. Play with the program preferences and options and the online help.

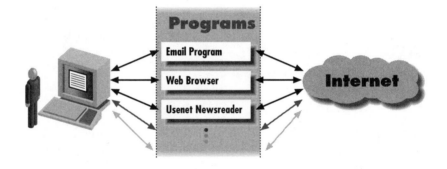

FIGURE 3-3

The Internet can be viewed as a collection of programs

- *A Web search engine.* Better yet, get familiar with two or three. Each one works a little differently, as we'll see in Chapter 5, and indexes a different set of information.

- *A Usenet newsreader.* True, many Web browsers will also let you read Usenet news, but dedicated newsreaders sometimes have additional search features for locating newsgroups of interest.

The better you can use these programs, the faster you'll be able to work, and the less time you'll waste.

VIEW 3: THE INTERNET IS A COLLECTION OF RESOURCES

Some Internet books present themselves as an index or Yellow Pages of the Net. If you want to find information on classical music, for example, you look up "Music, Classical" in the book, and the entry contains Web URLs, Usenet newsgroup names, and so on. These books promote a view that the Internet is a collection of resources, such as Web sites, newsgroups, and mailing lists. Since most people are familiar with telephone books, this view should feel natural.

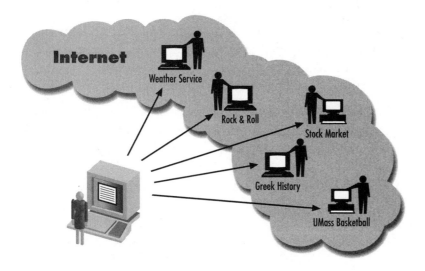

FIGURE 3-4
The Internet can be viewed as a collection of resources

Another advantage of this view is that somebody else—presumably an expert—has already done the work of locating great resources, so all you have to do is look them up. A Web search engine, in contrast, will show you a hundred resources and leave it to you to find the good ones.

The resource view has three disadvantages, however. First, as we said in the preface, Internet Yellow Pages quickly go out of date as the Net rapidly changes. (Look how many of their covers shout, "Newly updated!") Second, these books generally list only one or two resources for each topic. You don't have much choice. A telephone Yellow Pages lists every business in a geographical area. Internet Yellow Pages list only a tiny fraction. One hopes that the listed resources are the best ones, but one can't be sure, especially since the Net is always changing. Similarly, the topics themselves are limited. If you need information on champagne glasses but your Internet Yellow Pages has no listing, you're out of luck.

The third and most serious disadvantage, however, is that this view is limited to one topic at a time. A Yellow Pages can be good for looking up "classical music" or "stereo components," but it's useless for looking up "best stereo components for classical music." That is, Yellow Pages are lousy for finding *combinations* of topics.

YOU'LL DISCOVER RESOURCES AS YOU EXPLORE

This book doesn't focus on specific resources on the Net. It's not possible to predict each reader's areas of interest; even if it were possible, the Net would change and make any recommendations obsolete. Instead, this book tries to turn you into an effective searcher so you can find the best resources yourself.

This book does include an appendix, however, listing resources specially chosen to help you search. You may find them to be good starting points for further searching. For example, rather than list the Web sites of 100 companies, we list one Web site that specializes in locating companies.

URLS ARE WEB ADDRESSES

"A Beginner's Guide to URLs" can be found at *http://www.ncsa.uiuc.edu/ demoweb/url-primer.html.*

Resources on the Net are often identified by funny-looking names, called URLs (Uniform Resource Locators). Each link on a Web page represents a URL. Most browsers, in fact, will display the URL of a link if you position the mouse over the link without selecting it.

URLs have two parts: a type, and a location, separated by a colon. In Yahoo's URL:

http://www.yahoo.com

the "type" is *http* (HyperText Transfer Protocol), which is Net jargon meaning the resource is a Web page. The "location" is *//www. yahoo.com*, which means the Web page is located on the computer named *www.yahoo.com*.

Let's explore types and locations in more detail. Types describe the sort of information you'll see when you visit the URL with your Web browser. The most common types are shown in Table 3-1.

The form of the "location" part depends on the type. For instance, if the type is a Web page (*http*), then the location will have a computer name, optionally followed by the name of a file or directory (folder).

Type	Information you'll find
http	A typical Web page with text, graphics, sound, etc.
gopher	A Gopher menu.
ftp	An FTP site, with files for downloading.
news	A Usenet newsgroup.
mailto	An opportunity to send email.
telnet	A login connection to another machine.
file	A file on your computer.

TABLE 3-1: *Types of Internet resources*

If the type is a Usenet newsgroup (*news*), the location will be a news-group name. If the type is *mailto*, the location is an email address. Here are some more examples of URLs:

ftp://ftp.microsoft.com/Products/Windows/

gopher://spinaltap.micro.umn.edu

news:rec.arts.books

mailto:nuts@ora.com

To use the World Wide Web, it isn't necessary to understand URLs. All you need to know is how to tell your Web browser to connect to a particular URL. URLs are easier to remember, however, if you understand their parts.

If URLs don't make complete sense yet, don't worry. We'll explore them in more depth as the book goes on.

VIEW 4:
THE INTERNET IS
LIKE A LIBRARY

Libraries and the Net are both filled with information on many topics. In a library, you can leisurely browse through the stacks, examining whatever book catches your eye. Similarly, on the Net, you can wander from one Web page to another, following links that look interesting. In a library, you can use a card catalog or computer database to locate books directly by title, author, subject, or keywords. On the Internet, similarly, you can use a Web search engine to locate resources. Library books are identified by numbers (e.g., Dewey Decimal), and Internet documents are often identified by URLs.

Actually, the Internet is more like a huge collection of libraries scattered around the world. Each of these libraries, unfortunately, has its own method for organizing and accessing information. Worse, there is no master index of all the libraries and their contents. Instead, people have created dozens of indexes (Web search engines), all with different information, all organized differently, and all out of date in different ways.

It gets worse. There's no roadmap to get from one library to another. If you happen to know each library's street address (e.g., Web URL), you can get around, but if not, you'll be unaware of many libraries that might contain what you want. And the roads (network connections) between libraries are sometimes speedy, sometimes crowded and slow, and sometimes closed for repairs.

Finally, there are so many libraries that you can't possibly exhaust them all in one lifetime. A vital piece of information you desperately need could be sitting in some obscure corner of the Net, gathering dust, and you'd never know it.

Whew! Should we all give up, pack up our Web browsers, and go home? No, nothing quite so drastic. Given any topic, you can generally find *something* about it on the Net. You just aren't guaranteed that the information you find will be what you need. And if you follow the Internet Searcher's Rules for the Road (Chapter 1), your chances of finding what you need are greatly increased.

YOU CAN CONDUCT POWERFUL SEARCHES BY KEYWORD

When you're in a library and don't know where to find some information, it's common to ask a librarian. From a description of your goal, a librarian can often recommend a book or a relevant area of the library for your purposes.

On the Internet, a Web search engine plays the role of librarian. You describe what you're looking for in words, called *keywords*, that you give to the search engine. The search engine thinks for a while and responds with a list of Web resources that might contain relevant information. For example, to learn about the best stereo components for classical music, you might type:

```
stereo component AND classical music
```

This input is called a *query*. Note that queries can search for combinations of topics, which the resources view cannot handle conveniently. We'll cover queries in detail in Chapter 5.

An advantage of the library view is ease of use. There's very little memorization required. A disadvantage is that you have to wait for the search engine to find things. While search engines have become quite fast, it still takes time for you to connect to the search engine and wait for its results to reach your computer.

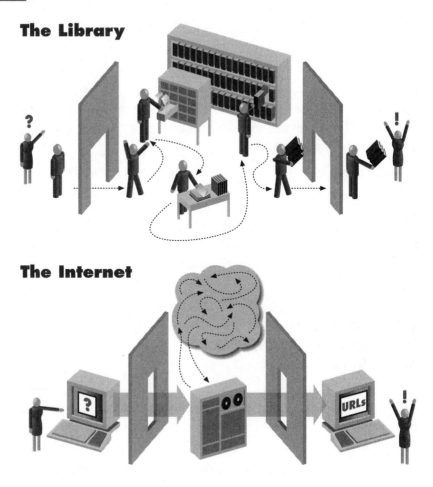

The Library

The Internet

FIGURE **3-5**
*The Internet can be
viewed as a library*

Another disadvantage is that search engines are loyal but dumb. They are perfectly happy to show you 250 responses to your search, where 225 of them are useless to you. (Librarians are much smarter!) Most search engines attempt to rank their responses from best to worst, but these rankings are guesses at best. It's common to scan through 10–20 responses before choosing one that looks applicable.

A more subtle problem with the library view is that it portrays the Net as a passive tool that exists only to be consumed by the public. The Internet, however, is not passive: it's an active community. Many of the best Web sites were designed by volunteers purely out of the goodness of their hearts. You too can create an Internet resource, enhance your online reputation, and feel good about yourself. We'll discuss this in detail in Chapter 11.

CHOOSE THE VIEW THAT'S RIGHT FOR YOU

Each of the views of the Internet—as computers, programs, resources, or a library—may be used to search for information. Sometimes you'll switch between views in a single search. Table 3-2 summarizes the advantages and disadvantages of each view discussed in this chapter.

Here's an example of using some views we've discussed. Suppose you are doing research on ancient Greece and need some information. Where should you look? Since you don't know, you adopt the library view. You visit a Web search engine and enter the query Greek history. The search engine responds with thousands of links to documents that contain the words "Greek" and "history." It's hard to deal with that much information, so you try some more specific queries, follow a few likely looking links, and locate some things you need.

View As	Advantages	Disadvantages
Computers	Speed, if you know where to look.	May require memorization.
Programs	Good for browsing and organizing.	Doesn't provide guidance for searching.
Resources	Intuitive to use. Quickly narrows your search.	No combination of topics. May require memorization. Not all resources on a topic are equally good.
A Library	Simple, powerful searching: single topics, combinations.	Can be slow. Can find too much information. Hides the fact that the Net is an active community, not a passive tool.

TABLE 3-2
Views of the Internet

After a while, you run out of patience but still don't have enough information, so you adopt the resource view. The Web didn't give you what you need. What other resources exist? How about Usenet? Using your newsreader to search for newsgroups with "greek" in the name, you locate *soc.culture.greek* and post a question, asking where good online sources on Greek history can be found. A few hours later, someone responds that the machine *ftp.history.athens.gr* (a fictional name for this example) contains a treasure trove of information.

To reach this machine, you adopt the computer view. You connect directly to *ftp.history.athens.gr* and download the information using FTP.

How do you view the Internet?

- Although the Net is like a big encyclopedia, it's also uncensored and unedited, which makes it a bit of a grab bag. In the Frequently Asked Questions document for *rec.pets.dogs* on Usenet, there's as much space given to photographing black dogs as there is to housebreaking. I also think of the Net as a worldwide community; it gives me a warm feeling when I connect with somebody far away, or with a member of one of my online "families" (like serious basketball fans). —Ellie Cutler

- The Internet is a lot more than a library because it's constantly updated. Even if something on the Internet is old information, there's probably something newer somewhere that supercedes the old stuff. It's also a community. I remember when a mailing list member was killed in an airplane crash. The whole list was so shocked by her death that we collected $2,000 and donated it to a charitable cause she would have liked. I also explain the Net as "a bunch of computers connected by wires" to people who aren't Internet savvy, but I rarely think about it this way myself. —Fern Dickman

- The Internet is like a combination of a daily newspaper, a news radio station, a million retail shops, a huge college library, white and yellow pages, bulletin boards (both physical and electronic), meeting rooms/clubs/bars, and so on. —Harv Laser

1. Before you read this chapter, how did you view the Internet? Was your view similar to any of the four we discussed?

2. For each of the following items, which view do you think would be best for locating the item online?

   (a) Today's stock market prices

   (b) The Usenet newsgroup *misc.business.consulting*

   (c) Pictures of former United States presidents

   (d) A review of the movie *Star Wars*

   (e) Yahoo

3. Another way to view the Internet is as a giant community. When you need to find something, you can ask other users for guidance in locating popular resources.

   Can you think of some advantages and disadvantages of using this "community" view to search for something?

4. Can you think of any other ways to view the Internet? If so, how might these views be useful for searching?

Choosing an Effective Starting Point

4

The Internet does not have a single "starting point" for searching. It has many. Yahoo, which we saw in Chapter 1, is just one search engine out of hundreds, and each can locate only a portion of the material on the Internet. Thus, it's important to start your search at a place that is capable of leading you to your goal.

It's not possible to know in advance if you've chosen a good starting point, however. Therefore, it's important to become familiar with different kinds of starting points and their strengths and weaknesses. In this chapter, we'll introduce and compare:

- *Web search engines*: These provide a convenient way to locate on-line resources by topic or keyword.
- *Specialized Web sites*: These frequently lead to information not available from search engines.
- *FAQs*: Frequently Asked Questions documents provide a more focused way to begin your search.
- *Guessing*: As you gain intuition online, you'll learn to follow hunches to locate information quickly.
- *Discussion groups*: Knowledgeable users can point you in the right direction, as long as you aren't in a hurry.

Search the Net in Style
*http://www.cnet.com/
Resources/Tech/Advisers/
Search*

**Some hints and tips for
starting your search are
available at this Web site.**

WEB SEARCH ENGINES PROVIDE RAPID FEEDBACK

Web search engines are perhaps the quickest way to begin a search, as we saw in the Sherlock Holmes example in Chapter 1. Just connect to a search engine, type a few keywords, and in a few seconds (on a good day) you'll be looking at dozens or hundreds of information links.

As we also saw in Chapter 1, Web search engines aren't perfect. They can miss things and often locate irrelevant information. Chapter 5 will provide an in-depth discussion of techniques for effective Web searching with search engines.

GET TO KNOW SEVERAL WEB SEARCH ENGINES

Don't rely on a single search engine to find what you need. As we'll see later, each search engine is able to locate some, but not all, Web pages on the Internet. In addition, each search engine has a different combination of search features, frequency of updating its information, and speed. So if you can't find what you need using one Web search engine, try another. Below is a list of popular search engines and their locations.

AltaVista	*http://www.altavista.digital.com*
Excite	*http://www.excite.com*
HotBot	*http://www.hotbot.com*
InfoSeek	*http://www.infoseek.com*
Lycos	*http://www.lycos.com*
Magellan	*http://www.mckinley.com*
Open Text	*http://index.opentext.net*
WebCrawler	*http://www.webcrawler.com*
Yahoo	*http://www.yahoo.com*

I usually begin with AltaVista, because it is large and quick, or Yahoo, because its links are conveniently organized into categories. (This recommendation is subject to change as search engine technology improves.)

For up-to-date information, look at an online list of current search engines. See "Lists of Search Engines" in Appendix A.

What's your favorite search engine?

- Yahoo. I use more than one though. Even when I begin with the same keywords, I get different results from different search engines.

  Actually, the "search engine" I use most often is to snoop through the home pages of other people. Personal home pages invariably contain really interesting links. —Kathleen Callaway

- I used to use WebCrawler, which I found gave a lot more info than Lycos, but now I use AltaVista instead. Sometimes I'll use more than one if I want to make sure I've covered everything. —Ellie Cutler

- AltaVista. The fill-in-the-blanks form is right there on the first page so I don't have to scroll down looking for it. I also like the summaries that it prints for each hit. I can usually tell from the first few lines whether the hit is relevant or not. —Fern Dickman

- I've tried many search engines but have been disappointed with the results, so I tend to use other methods. If I have a question on a particular topic, I'll search for a mailing list on that topic and scan through the old postings, looking for people who seem to be experts. Then I'll send the question directly to an expert by email, trying to phrase it as clearly as possible. Most people I reach are pretty helpful.

  I also receive email of this type—questions from other users— and am usually able to help out, either by giving the name of someone else to contact or by forwarding the message to someone I know. —Robert Strandh

---

META-SEARCH ENGINES CAN SAVE TIME

A special kind of Web search engine, called a *meta-search engine*, lets you use several search engines at once. Instead of doing a search itself, a meta-search engine sends your request to other search engines, collects the results, and presents them to you. This is generally faster than using several search engines manually.

We'll discuss meta-search engines in depth in Chapter 5, but for now, try experimenting with some of the more popular ones:

MetaCrawler   *http://metacrawler.cs.washington.edu*

SavvySearch   *http://guaraldi.cs.colostate.edu:2000/*

A more up-to-date list of meta-search engines and related pages can be found on Yahoo:

*http://www.yahoo.com/Computers_and_Internet/Internet/
World_Wide_Web/Searching_the_Web/All_in_One_Search_Pages/*

SPECIALIZED SITES PROVIDE UNIQUE, FOCUSED INFORMATION

Sometimes people create detailed, comprehensive Web sites devoted to specific topics: an area of science, a genre of literature, an occupation, a well-known organization, and so on. Such *specialized Web sites* may contain answers you are seeking, but more importantly for this chapter, they frequently provide access to related online resources and therefore can serve as effective starting points. Some of them even contain specialized search engines that focus on the topic at hand, and which have access to information unavailable to more general search engines.

Specialized Web sites are often the second place that you search. First, you use a regular Web search engine to locate a specialized site related to your topic. Then you use the specialized site's links or internal search engine to locate the information you seek. For example, if you're looking for information on how to repair the furnace in your home, you might use a Web search engine to locate a site devoted to homeowner's issues. That specialized site may then have a database of home repair tips to be searched.

A GOOD GUESS IS WORTH A THOUSAND SEARCHES

Sometimes the quickest way to find something is to guess its location. In Chapter 3, when discussing the viewpoint that the Internet is a bunch of computers, we saw that Microsoft's computer names end with *microsoft.com*, so we located their Web site at *www.microsoft.com* without needing to search. This kind of name-guessing can cut down your search time drastically.

As you gain experience using the Internet, you'll develop instincts for locating things. If a Web search engine doesn't find a page devoted to your topic, you might explore other pages that are marginally related and eventually lead you to more relevant resources. For instance, suppose your cat is sick and you need veterinary information. A Web search, however, doesn't locate the information you seek. You might try beginning a new search at a general pet information site, a cat food company's site, or even a Web page on dogs in the hope that you'll be led toward information on cats.

This book is designed to help you become a good guesser. When we discuss finding Web page locations, computer names, email addresses and so on in other chapters, we give pointers on how to improve your guessing skills. The quiz questions in each chapter also give you practice in following your hunches.

FAQS PROVIDE INTRODUCTORY INFORMATION AND POINTERS

An *FAQ*, or *Frequently Asked Questions* document, is a list of common questions and their answers. (Some people pronounce FAQ as "F-A-Q," and others say "fack." In this book, we write "an FAQ" according to the first pronunciation.) Hundreds of FAQs are available on the Internet, each devoted to a particular topic: air travel, juggling, computer viruses, antique cars, Bulgarian culture, and so on. FAQs are created by interested people—usually volunteers—who have noticed the same questions being asked repeatedly in online discussion groups.

A well-written FAQ is a terrific starting point. Even if it doesn't answer your question directly, an FAQ is likely to contain pointers to further collections of information found on Web pages and other online resources. A good set of pointers can significantly cut down your search time.

Sadly, FAQs are often ignored or forgotten by Internet searchers. Don't pass them up; when you need an answer online, one of your first steps should be to look for an FAQ. Large collections of FAQs are available at:

http://www.cis.ohio-state.edu/hypertext/faq/usenet/top.html

ftp://rtfm.mit.edu/pub/usenet-by-hierarchy/

http://www.lib.ox.ac.uk/internet/news/

Each of these collections has many of the same FAQs, but presented with a different user interface.

FAQs are also posted on Usenet, both in specific newsgroups relevant to the FAQ topic, and more general "answers" newsgroups with names ending in *.answers*: *comp.answers* for computer-related FAQs, *rec.answers* for recreation-related FAQs, and so on. FAQs are generally posted at least once a month, often on the first day of the month.

If no FAQ has been written on a topic, consider writing one yourself, turning your experience into a useful reference for your fellow Internet citizens. Chapter 11 discusses how to do this.

LOOK FOR AN FAQ BEFORE POSTING PUBLIC QUESTIONS

If you are considering asking a question in a public discussion group, read the group's FAQ first, if one exists. If people don't read the FAQ and keep posting common questions over and over, the discussion group suffers in two ways:

- The discussion group becomes cluttered with repeated responses that become boring for most readers.
- Long-time readers start leaving when they become bored with seeing the same questions posted. As a result, fewer experts will be around to answer questions.

Checking the FAQ will speed up your search and also help you avoid embarrassment. If you post a question that happens to be answered in the FAQ, be prepared for terse or rude responses like "Read the FAQ," "That's question 23.4 in the FAQ," or even "RTFM," which stands for "Read The Fine Manual." (Actually, the word isn't "Fine," but this is a G-rated book.)

DISCUSSION GROUPS PROVIDE A FORUM FOR QUESTIONS

Another way to locate something, if you are not in a hurry, is to post a question in a public discussion group, like a Usenet newsgroup, or a forum run by your online service provider. If the discussion group is active, you might receive an answer within a few hours; if not, it might take days.

Be sure to post your question in an appropriate group. Usenet, for example, has well over 18,000 newsgroups at press time, so choosing the right newsgroup may be difficult. Before posting, take some time and read the newsgroup to see what kinds of topics are covered. You can also check the Usenet Info Center:

http://sunsite.unc.edu/usenet-i/

which describes the focus of many newsgroups. See the section "Newsreaders can locate newsgroup names" for more help in locating newsgroups of interest.

Don't feel obligated to post your question to the whole group. After you've read a discussion group for a while, the participants will become familiar to you, so you might try emailing a question directly to a user who seems knowledgeable. Make your question as short and to-the-point as possible, so the user can understand it quickly and not have to ask for clarification. Be polite, and be sure to email a thank-you note afterwards. (Few people do.)

NEWSREADERS CAN LOCATE NEWSGROUP NAMES

Usenet newsgroup names indicate their topics, as we discussed in Chapter 2. So, to locate an appropriate newsgroup, search for one with an appropriate-sounding name. (Even if the name sounds right, however, don't post blindly into the newsgroup. Read the newsgroup for a while before posting anything, to avoid the embarrassment of an off-topic post.)

Different newsreaders use different commands for locating newsgroup names. Suppose you want to search for a newsgroup with the word "opera" in its name. Here's how to do it with many popular newsreaders.

How to Find the Right Place to Post

http://www.cis. ohio-state.edu/hypertext/ faq/usenet/finding-groups/ general/faq.html

Tips on finding the right Usenet newsgroup for posting are found at this FAQ.

- *America Online*: Enter keyword `newsgroups`, and select Search All Newsgroups. A window will appear, allowing you to search for newsgroups by topic. Type `opera` and press RETURN.

- *CompuServe*: `GO USENET` and select Usenet Newsreader. From the Usenet Newsgroups menu, choose Subscribe to Newsgroups. The Subscribe to Newsgroups window appears. In the space provided, type `opera` and select the Search button.

  Note that this search checks not only newsgroup names, but also newsgroup descriptions. For instance, if a newsgroup description happens to contain the word "operate," it would match "opera."

- *Emacs GNUS*: Type `AM` to invoke the command `gnus-group-list-all-matching`. When prompted, type `opera` and press RETURN.
  If your GNUS version is too old to support the above command, type `j` to invoke the command `gnus-group-jump-to-group`. Press the space bar. A buffer will be created containing the names of all available newsgroups. (This may take some time.) When the buffer appears, use normal Emacs search commands to search for `opera`.

- *Free Agent*: Select the Group Pane and choose Show All Groups from the Group menu. Then choose Find from the Edit menu. Type `opera` in the space provided and press RETURN.

- *Gravity*: From the Newsgroup menu, select Subscribe. In the Search box, type `opera`.

- *Microsoft Network*: From the Communicate menu, choose Internet Community. Select Internet News Groups, then Try Newsgroups Now, then the Newsgroups button. In the space provided, labeled "Display newsgroups which contain," type `opera`.

- *Microsoft News*: Select Newsgroups. In the box that appears, type `opera`.

- *Netscape News*: There's no convenient way to search for newsgroup names. You're better off visiting the Usenet Info Center on the Web, described below. You can browse around looking for a relevant-looking newsgroup. From the Options menu, select Show All Newsgroups and rummage through the folders.

- *nn*: Type the G command. When prompted for a newsgroup name, type opera and press RETURN. For each newsgroup containing the word "opera," you'll be asked if you want to read it. Respond y for yes or n for no.

- *rn*: At the prompt:

  ```
  read now? [ynq]
  ```

  type:

  ```
  l opera
  ```

  and press RETURN. If the search finds a newsgroup (in this case, *rec.music.opera*) and you want to subscribe, type:

  ```
  g rec.music.opera
  ```

  and press RETURN.

- *Prodigy*: Enter the jumpword usenet and select Explore News-groups. Press the Find Newsgroups button and then select Search Newsgroups for Text Pattern Below. In the space provided, type opera and press RETURN.

- *tin*: Type y to yank in all newsgroups, and type / to initiate a search. At the prompt, type opera and press RETURN.

- *trn*: Same as for rn.

- *Trumpet*: In the Group menu, select Subscribe. In the box labeled Search, type opera. (Do not press RETURN.)

- *xrn*: In Newsgroup mode, type g (the ngGoto command), and in the box that appears, type opera.

To search for a newsgroup name containing a different word, simply replace opera above with the word of your choice.

If none of these methods works for you, try connecting to the Usenet Info Center:

http://sunsite.unc.edu/usenet-i/

and browsing around to locate newsgroups of interest.

SOME SEARCH ENGINES CATALOG USENET NEWS

A related method for beginning a search is to use a *Usenet search engine*. These search engines collect large numbers of Usenet news articles, index them, and allow searching by keyword. If anybody has had a discussion on Usenet recently (or even long ago) about your topic of interest, you can locate it and perhaps get a pointer to more information. This technique can be faster than posting a question of your own.

Currently, the most popular Usenet search engines and their locations are:

AltaVista	*http://www.altavista.digital.com*
Deja News	*http://www.dejanews.com*

At press time, AltaVista stores several weeks' worth of recent Usenet news, deleting old articles as new ones arrive. Deja News does not delete articles and has the more ambitious goal of—someday—storing all known Usenet news.

By the way, Usenet search engines can be a quick way to find FAQs, since many FAQs are posted on Usenet. For instance, to locate an FAQ for Macintosh computers, you could search for `macintosh faq` on Deja News.

| **Case Study: Finding a recipe** | ▪ I entered `"chocolate cake"` `+recipe` at AltaVista and got hundreds of hits in two seconds. —Harv Laser |
| | ▪ Using my news-reading program, I searched for a Usenet news-group on food and found *rec.food.recipes*. From there, I found the recipe archives maintained by the readers of the newsgroup. —Kathleen Callaway |

CHOOSE WISELY

It's unlikely the Internet will have a comprehensive table of contents any time soon. Thus, the speed and success of a search will depend on one's choice of starting point. Table 4-1 summarizes the benefits of the starting points discussed in this chapter.

Type	Strengths	Weaknesses
Search engine	Can be fast.	Irrelevant information can overwhelm useful information. (Good choice of keywords can help here.)
Specialized Web site	Leads to information inaccessible to search engines.	May not exist for your topic.
FAQ	A great place to start.	Not all topics have FAQs.
Guess	Can be very fast.	Requires experience, intuition.
Discussion group	Reaches a community of experts. (But read the FAQ first.)	Relatively slow. Experts may tire of beginner questions. Non-experts may reply with wrong or incomplete information.

TABLE 4-1
Starting points

QUIZ: Choosing an effective starting point

1. Try out some Web search engines mentioned in this chapter. Take note of similarities and differences. Which ones do you like best?

2. Can you locate Usenet newsgroups devoted to the following topics?

   (a) Physics

   (b) Tropical fish

   (c) Video games

   (d) Job announcements

   (e) Your favorite hobby

   (f) Your religion

3. Use Deja News to locate an FAQ on investment.

4. Another way to start a search is to ask a knowledgeable colleague. Do you think this is an effective way to start a search, compared to the methods we've discussed in this chapter? Why or why not?

5. Can you think of another kind of starting point not mentioned in this chapter?

Web Searching Techniques

5

Web search engines are a popular and powerful means for locating information on the Internet. Most of them are designed to be easy to use for basic searching. Just type a few words that represent the concept you want to find, press a button (usually labeled Search or Go), and view the results, as we saw in Chapter 1. For many Web users, this is what searching is all about.

Unfortunately, "easy to use" doesn't mean that the search engine will find what you want. To be an effective Net searcher, you might sometimes need to look beyond the friendly-looking graphical interface and apply more powerful search techniques. In this chapter, we will cover:

- Search engines: what they do, and how they work.
- Three types of search engines, and reasons for using (or not using) each type.
- Simple queries, a basic searching technique. (Plus a few reasons why simple queries are less simple than they appear.)
- Advanced queries, a more powerful searching technique that uses "operators" to focus your search.
- General search strategies to help guide you toward your goal.
- A brief overview of Gopher search.

SEARCH ENGINES LOOK UP WEB PAGES IN CATALOGS

When you ask a search engine to locate information, what actually happens? Does the search engine scan the whole Internet, looking for relevant Web pages? No, that would be terribly time-consuming. A single request would take weeks.

Catalog

The set of Web pages that a search engine knows how to find. Also called a *database* or *index*.

Instead, a search engine keeps a list of all the Web pages that it knows about. This list is called the *catalog* of the search engine. Rather than scanning the whole Internet, a search engine looks in its catalog to locate pages.

Catalogs are like telephone books. When we need somebody's phone number, we don't run through town, following telephone wires and peeking into people's homes. We just look up the number in the phone book. Similarly, search engines look up Web pages in their catalogs.

Note that a search engine can find only the Web pages in its catalog. This is one reason why some search engines find what you want, but others don't—their catalogs cover different sets of pages. No catalog covers the entire Internet (despite any hype to the contrary). The Internet keeps changing, so catalogs are never completely up to date. Thus, if a search engine says it can't find something, your desired information might still be somewhere on the Internet. It's just not in the catalog of that particular search engine.

GIVE A QUERY, GET A HIT

Keyword

A word, partial word, or phrase that you can give to a search engine. Also called a *search term*.

Now that we have explained catalogs briefly, let's define some more terms. The words that you give to a search engine are called *keywords*. A keyword can be a word, like `alligator`, or part of a word, like `allig`. You can even treat a phrase as a single keyword, as in `sharpened alligator teeth`.

Query

One or more keywords that, together, represent the concept that you want to find on the Net. Also called a *search string*.

A set of one or more keywords is called a *query*. A query represents a complete statement to a search engine, describing what you want to find. (Keywords in a query can be connected in various ways, as we'll see when we talk about *operators*. Here's an advance peek at a query with operators: `reptile AND dental work AND NOT sharpened alligator teeth`.)

If a search engine finds a page in its catalog that matches your query, the matching page is called a *hit*. A successful query leads to one or many hits, whereas an unsuccessful query—one that matches nothing in the catalog—yields no hits.

Hit
A Web page in the catalog that matches your query. Also called a *match*.

Case Study: Find stock prices

- I queried AltaVista with `New York Stock Exchange` and found its official page at *nyse.com*. —Ellie Cutler
- I tried the query `new york stock exchange` on AltaVista and got back a ton of hits. After checking the first few hits, one of them took me to a page at Ohio State's business school, where I could type a ticker symbol and get back the current price. —Fern Dickman
- I went to Yahoo and used the keyword `NYSE` to search for the New York Stock Exchange. This located a Web site displaying a daily summary of trading. —Kathleen Callaway
- I started at CNN's Web page, *http://cnn.com*, and followed their Financial Market link. —Harv Laser
- I used Lycos to search for the Stockholm Stock Exchange, where I have some shares, and found it. —Robert Strandh

SEARCH ENGINES BUILD THEIR CATALOGS IN DIFFERENT WAYS

How do search engines learn about other Web pages? They generally use one of three techniques to build their catalogs of Web page information. The techniques are called active, passive, and meta-search.

An *active* search engine collects Web page information by itself. It uses a program called a *spider* (also called a *robot*, *wanderer* or *crawler*) that travels around the Net, locates Web pages, and adds entries to the catalog. Some spiders run all the time, adding information to the catalog on a regular basis. Others run less frequently, perhaps updating the catalog weekly or monthly.

Some people think their home pages are private if they don't tell anybody the URL, or if they tell it only to a few friends. But then a spider finds it, and one day they get email from a stranger, commenting on their Web page. Surprise!

In contrast, a *passive* search engine does not seek out Web pages by itself. It learns about new Web pages only when told about them.

Robots, Wanderers, and Spiders
http://info.webcrawler.com/ mak/projects/robots/ robots.html

More information about spiders, robots, and wanderers can be found at this Web site.

Passive search engines allow people to *register* their Web pages, usually by filling out a form online. Once a page is registered with the search engine, the page can be found by queries.

Some search engines have both active and passive features. They use a spider to gather information, but they also allow users to register pages. (Most active search engines, in fact, have a registration feature.)

Eureka Search Engine
http://www.best.com/ ~mentorms/e_sedef.htm

A discussion of the difference between passive and active search engines (called "directories" and "robots," respectively) is found at this site.

The third type of search engine is the *meta-search* engine. Meta-search engines don't catalog any Web pages themselves. Instead, they forward users' queries to other search engines to do the actual work. When results come back from the other search engines, the meta-search engine presents them to the user, possibly summarizing them or at least giving them a consistent appearance.

Each type of search engine has strengths and weaknesses. Active search engines tend to have large catalogs because their spiders are always gathering information about new Web pages. Active catalogs are also generally updated sooner than passive ones, since active catalogs update themselves and don't rely on humans for the information. Without human supervision, however, this automatic cataloging isn't always done well. An active search engine is more likely to give you more hits than necessary in response to a query. If the extra hits are irrelevant, they're a waste of time to wade through, but even relevant hits are a problem if you get too many of them. A spider may catalog every page at a Web site, not just the "main" page, so your search results could be filled with relevant pages from the same site without indicating which page is the main one.

Passive search engines have the potential to be very organized. When users register a page, they can describe its contents in great detail. As a result, the search engine administrators can catalog the page carefully so it'll be found by appropriate searches. One drawback, however, is that the administrators might catalog the page in a way that's natural for them but unexpected for you. For instance, you won't find anything under `lawyers` if the administrators have filed the information under `attorneys` or `legal resources`. In addition, the catalogs of passive search engines tend to be smaller than those available to active and meta-search engines, since passive engines rely on human input (registration) to build their catalogs. Finally, passive catalogs get out of date quickly if users don't update the registered information.

1 *Active Search Engine*

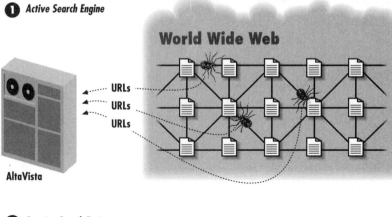

2 *Passive Search Engine*

3 *Meta-search Engine*

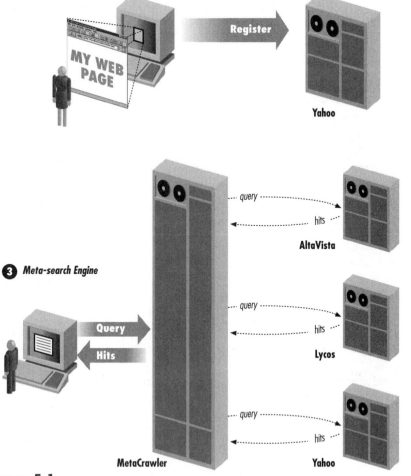

FIGURE **5-1**
How search engines build their catalogs

What are some shortcomings of search engines?	■ The way they sort and rate info. Sometimes the useless info ends up at the top of the list. —Ellie Cutler
	■ Often you get too many hits: hundreds, perhaps thousands. Then you have to scroll through them to find one or two relevant ones. So it helps to know how to narrow your search using a particular engine's advanced query language: when to put quotes around keywords, when to use operators like AND and OR, and so on. —Harv Laser
	■ Well, bless their hearts, they try hard, but they really can't distinguish word meanings. I mean, they can hardly tell a (graphics) card from a (playing) card. —Kathleen Callaway
	■ Some don't catalog some important areas of the Net, like Gopher and FTP sites. Also, each search engine works differently, so you have to invest some time understanding how each one works. —Bob Parker

Meta-search engines have a big advantage; they query many search engines simultaneously, saving you work. The main disadvantage is longer search time. If you need results quickly, you might not want to wait for a meta-search engine to query a dozen other search engines. (But experiment with several meta-search engines, since some are faster than others.) Another disadvantage is that the meta-search engine may summarize the data it receives, or it might present only the first few matches from each search engine, possibly hiding information that could be helpful or relevant. Table 5-1 summarizes the strengths and weaknesses of the three types of search engines.

When choosing or using a search engine, take a moment and find out (if possible) whether the engine uses active, passive, or meta-search techniques. The dividing lines are becoming blurred, however. Some passive engines, such as Yahoo, now query other engines

Type	Strengths	Weaknesses
Active	Larger catalog.	Too many hits.
Passive	Possibly more organized.	Smaller catalog; items may be cataloged in unexpected places.
Meta-search	One query goes a long way.	Longer search time.

TABLE 5-1
Types of search engines

after a failed search, giving them restricted meta-search capabilities. Many active engines also allow pages to be registered manually, a feature of passive engines.

SIMPLE QUERIES ARE QUICK AND DIRTY

Now that we've covered the basics of search engines, let's discuss how to find things. The easiest way is to type a few keywords and do a search. This is called doing a *simple query*. For example, suppose you need some income tax information. To do a simple query, you could connect to a search engine, type the keywords `income tax` as your query, and press the Search button. In response, the search engine would present you with a list of hits.

Simple queries are good because they don't require much thinking: you can do them in the middle of a hectic day without distracting yourself from other tasks. On the down side, simple queries may be too broad, resulting in large numbers of hits, many of them unrelated to your goal. Our simple `income tax` query could easily yield 100,000 hits, including not only income tax regulations, but also home pages of people who happen to be tax auditors, essays on the Bulgarian tax system, and the lyrics to "Tax Man" by the Beatles. (Try it!)

CHOOSE YOUR KEYWORDS WITH CARE

The success of a Web search depends heavily on the keywords you choose. Spending a few moments formulating your search, rather than leaping onto a search engine, will save you time in the long run. Hastily chosen keywords may lead to large numbers of irrelevant hits that could have been avoided by more careful wording.

In addition, be sure to watch out for:

- *Misspellings*. Search engines use whatever you give them. If you misspell a keyword, a search engine will happily search for nonsense. Interestingly enough, a misspelled word may accidentally get relevant hits if people misspell the same word on their Web pages. Try searching for `recepe` instead of `recipe` and see what you get.

- *Alternate spellings.* Some words can be spelled in various ways: gray and grey, adaptor and adapter, and so on. Watch out for British spellings too (e.g., color vs. colour). Use the OR operator (described soon) to prevent the search from missing relevant matches: for example, color OR colour.

- *Synonyms.* If you want information on cars, should you search for car, automobile, or motor vehicle? Different Web pages may use different terms for the same concepts. As with alternate spellings, use the OR operator between these keywords.

- *Word forms.* In Chapter 1, we speculated on the difference between searching for poison or poisonous. The form of a word may matter significantly when doing a search. In particular, you may get different results if you search for a word or its plural (e.g., car vs. cars). In general, search for the singular, not the plural.

These issues will become less important as search engine technology improves. Some search engines can already avoid misspellings and recognize alternate word forms.

SIMPLE QUERIES AREN'T ALWAYS SIMPLE

Another problem with simple queries is that they look simpler than they really are. Different search engines treat simple queries in a variety of ways. If you aren't aware of the differences, then your simple query might produce unexpected results.

In the previous example, we constructed a simple query, income tax. Depending on which search engine you use, this simple query can mean different things and yield different results. Here are some examples of what different search engines might give you:

- Pages containing the *complete phrase* "income tax."

- Pages containing both the word "income" and the word "tax," located *near* each other.

- Pages containing both "income" and "tax," appearing *anywhere* on the Web page, in any order.

- Pages containing *either* the word "income" *or* the word "tax."

■ Pages related to the *concept* of income tax, but not necessarily containing the words "income" or "tax."

If your intention were to search for "income tax" as a phrase, some of these results would not be very helpful. In particular, the fourth type of behavior (either/or) would probably lead to many irrelevant hits. Sometimes, however, this "either/or" behavior is just what we want. Suppose we wanted to look up information on stereo equipment. We could use the query `stereo CD cassette tuner amplifier` in the hopes that the search engine would find Web pages containing at least some of these terms.

The moral is: if you use simple queries, it's a good idea to find out how they are treated by the search engine you use. You'll probably find documentation on the search engine's main Web page. Look for a link labeled Help, Options, or Search Tips.

ADVANCED QUERIES HELP TO FOCUS YOUR SEARCH

Fortunately, there's more to life than simple queries. *Advanced queries* can reduce irrelevant hits by making a query more specific. To do this, advanced queries may have *operators* to include and exclude keywords from the search. Operators are words or symbols that tell the search engine to treat your keywords in a special way. For example, if you wanted to look up income tax information for the United States, an advanced query might look like this:

`"income tax" AND ("United States" OR USA OR America)`

The operators in this query are AND, OR, parentheses, and quotation marks. The query says to search for the phrase `income tax` whenever it appears on the same page with `United States`, `USA`, or `America`. This advanced query is an attempt to limit the search to USA-specific tax information. Will the query work as expected? Probably not exactly. Some relevant pages might not mention the United States, and some irrelevant pages might coincidentally refer to the USA. But it's a start, and the operators are likely to eliminate some irrelevant hits.

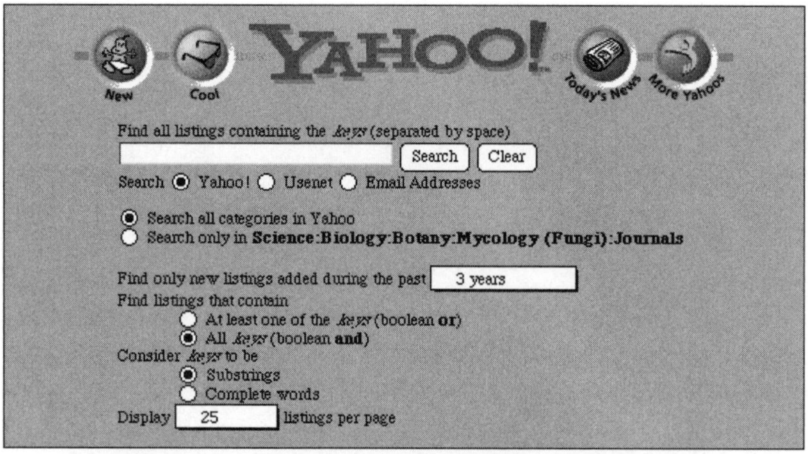

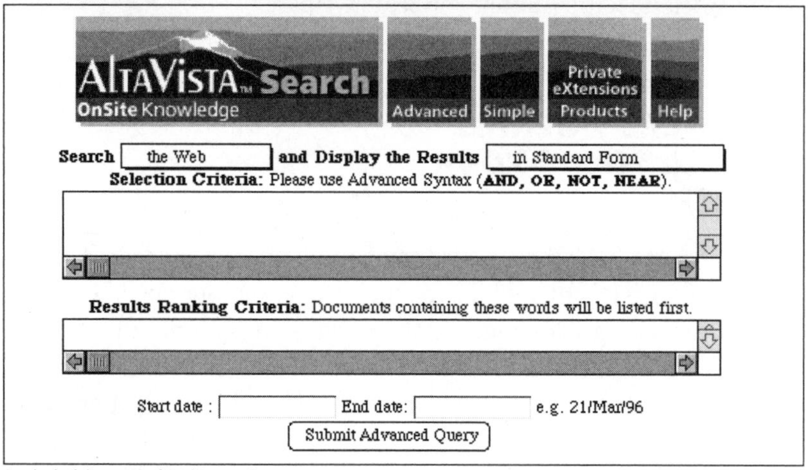

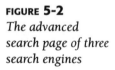

Reproduced with the permission of Digital Equipment Corporation.

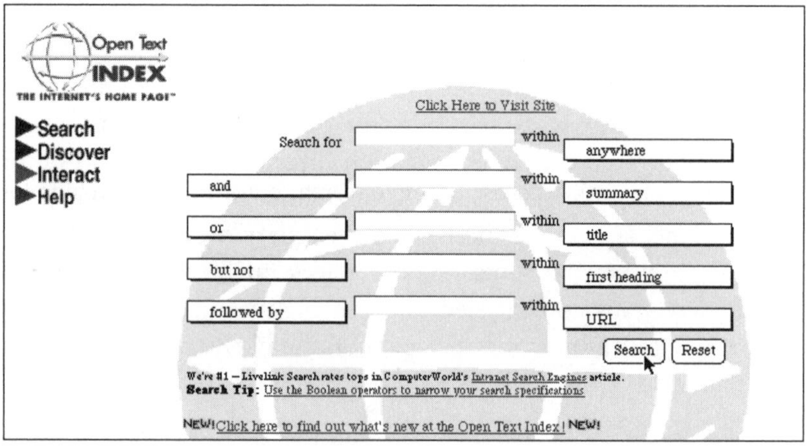

FIGURE 5-2

The advanced search page of three search engines

The operators in an advanced query are used to combine keywords in various ways. In the example, the AND operator indicates that keywords must all appear, and OR indicates choice. Quotation marks are used to group the words of a phrase as a single keyword, and parentheses are used to group keywords and operators so they are matched in a particular order. The types of operators supported by a search engine make up its *query language*.

ADVANCED QUERIES HAVE MANY FORMS

There is no standard query language on the Web, so each search engine may support different operators. The example in the previous section shows what an advanced query might look like, but some search engines will not understand it. Table 5-2 shows some common operators and how they usually appear, but remember that an advanced query meaningful to one search engine might be gibberish to another. Perhaps someday there will be a standard language for advanced queries, but for now, people must learn each search engine's language separately or avoid learning them by using a meta-search engine.

In this book, we'll use the operators AND, OR, NOT, quotation marks, and parentheses as given in Table 5-2.

Do you prefer simple or advanced queries?

- I start with a simple query. This gives me an idea of the amount of available information. From there, I narrow the list with increasingly advanced queries until I have a manageable list of hits. —Michael Rosencrantz

- It depends on how focused my topic is. If I were searching for info on law schools, I'd use a simple search, but if I were searching for the text of a specific law statute, I'd use advanced search. —Bob Parker

- I use the simple search on AltaVista 99 percent of the time. I'm not a math weenie, so that operator stuff sometimes confuses me. Each time I want to use operators, I read the online help again to see how. —Harv Laser

Concept	Appearance	Meaning
And	AND, &, &&	Match *all* of these keywords.
Or	OR, |, ||	Match *at least one* of these keywords.
Not	NOT, ~ , –	Match if this keyword is *not present.*
Some	Usually an on/off switch	Only *some* of the keywords must be matched.
Required keyword	+	Along with the "Some" operator, indicates a keyword that *must* be matched.
Near	NEAR	Match these keywords if they are *near each other.*
Adjacent	"quotation marks"	Match these keywords if they are *next to each other, in order.*
Grouping	(parentheses)	Try to match these keywords *before* matching the rest of the keywords. (Just as parentheses are used to group operations together in mathematics.)
Allow misspellings	Usually an on/off switch	Match words that are *almost the same spelling* as these keywords.
Allow partial words	Usually an on/off switch	Also called substring match. Match words that *contain* your keyword. For example, the keyword self would match both "myself" and "selfish".
Case sensitivity	Usually an on/off switch	Ignore or obey *capitalization* when matching words.
Wildcard	*	Match *anything*; for example, micro* would match words that begin with "micro".
Limit search	Usually an on/off switch	Search only *part* of the search engine's catalog.

TABLE 5-2
Advanced query operators

LEARN AN ADVANCED QUERY LANGUAGE ONLINE

It's a good idea to know the advanced query language of one or two search engines, but don't waste your time memorizing it. If a search engine has an advanced query language, the language is invariably documented on the search engine's Web site. Look for a link on the simple query page labeled Search Options, Advanced Options, Syntax, Boolean Operators, Search Tips, or something similar. (Don't confuse this documentation with the online help offered by your Web browser. For instance, Netscape Navigator has a Help menu that leads to documentation about the browser itself.)

Don't be afraid to practice with the advanced query language. You can't damage anything, and if you use the query language incorrectly, the worst you'll get is an error message.

SIMPLE QUERIES HAVE INVISIBLE, DEFAULT OPERATORS

Earlier, we saw that the simple query income tax could be interpreted in various ways by different search engines. It might mean income AND tax, or perhaps income OR tax, or even income NEAR tax. In other words, even though you don't use any operators in a simple query, the search engine will pretend that AND, OR, NEAR, or perhaps some other operator applies between your keywords. This invisible operator is called the *default operator* of a search engine, because the operator is automatically assumed to be present.

Some search engines let you change the default operator. In other words, if the default operator is OR—so the query income tax actually means income OR tax—you can change the default operator so income tax will mean income AND tax instead. It's usually simpler, however, just to do an advanced query with the operator you want.

Working with limited resources

If your computer has a relatively slow processor, a small amount of memory or hard disk space, or a slow modem, these factors may make searching the Net inconvenient or difficult. Here are some tips to speed up your search.

- *Turn off image loading.* Most Web browsers have an option to turn off graphics. Graphic images can be very time-consuming to load and display if your computer or network connection is slow. (Some Web pages will not function well without their graphics, however.)

- *Use a text-based browser.* A text-based Web browser, such as lynx, will start up faster and run faster than traditional browsers because it ignores all graphics. On the other hand, text-based browsers generally don't use the mouse, so you'll have to memorize keyboard commands to navigate the Net.

- *Make a home page on your hard drive.* When you run a browser, if your home page is out on the Internet somewhere, it can take time to load and view it. Instead, make a home page right on your local computer's hard drive. (Consult the browser's documentation to locate the command or option to select your home page. Some browsers, like Netscape Navigator, will let you turn your bookmark file into a Web page.) A local home page will cause the Web browser to start up much more quickly, since it needn't access the Internet to load the home page. If you also have a home page out on the Internet, make a bookmark to it (discussed in in Chapter 10) so you can access it conveniently.

- *Use the Back button.* The Back button of your Web browser returns you to the previously viewed page. Some Web pages provide a link to a previous page, but the Back button often produces faster results.

SEARCH STRATEGIES HELP YOU USE QUERIES EFFECTIVELY

Simple and advanced queries are tools that let you search for topics of interest. Unfortunately, they are *only* tools. They don't provide guidance. A hammer doesn't automatically make its owner into a carpenter. Similarly, queries don't automatically make people into expert Net searchers. It's time for the next step: learning how to *use* queries effectively.

The rest of this chapter is devoted to *search strategies*, general techniques for creating and using queries to find what you want. You

- *Use the Stop button.* The Stop button of your Web browser stops a page from loading. If you get tired of waiting for a large graphic image to load, select Stop. Many browsers will then display the text of the entire page, minus the graphics, allowing you to select links on the page.

- *Upgrade your hardware.* This is the most expensive option, but with hardware prices dropping like crazy, it's within reach of some users. Consider upgrading your:

  - *Network connection*: A faster modem means that all Internet access will be quicker.

  - *RAM*: More RAM allows more programs to run simultaneously, and allows your Web browser to have a larger cache, which speeds up access to Web sites you've previously visited. (Caching is explained in Chapter 10.)

  - *Hard drive*: A larger drive allows your Web browser to cache more images, meaning that previously loaded graphics will be re-displayed more quickly.

  - *Processor*: A faster CPU means that programs will start up faster and run faster, and disk access speed may increase.

On the other hand, if you have tons of RAM, CPU power, and/or networking speed, take advantage of it. Try running several Web browser windows at once, performing simultaneous searches in each.

won't find these search strategies listed on search pages. They're methods that work inside your head. We'll cover:

- *General search*, for when you know little about your topic.

- *Specific search*, for when you know a lot about your topic.

- *Incremental search*, for zeroing in on your topic.

- *Substring search*, for matching several similar keywords at once.

- *Search-and-jump*, a speedy, two-part search technique.

- *Category search*, for convenient browsing of a topic area.

- *Search-and-rank*, for locating the most relevant hits first.

Most of these search strategies can be used with any search engine, and each has advantages and disadvantages that we'll summarize at the end of the chapter.

GENERAL SEARCHES ARE BROAD BUT BLIND

Sometimes you have a general idea of what you want to find, but not a lot of details. A *general search* is a reliable way to search broadly for information online. A general search makes use of the advanced query operator OR to join keywords together, telling the search engine to locate pages that contain *any* of the keywords. The more keywords you add, the broader the search, and the more hits you are likely to get.

For example, suppose you want general information on federal income tax. A general search query might be:

```
"income tax" OR taxes OR IRS OR "Internal Revenue Service"
```

General search is also good for handling alternate spellings and synonyms, as we saw earlier. Just combine the words with OR, and the query will match pages containing any of the words.

If your search is very general, the odds are good that you'll get a relevant hit, but you may also get many irrelevant hits that bury the desired information from view.

General search works well together with *search-and-jump*, discussed later.

SPECIFIC SEARCHES PROVIDE QUICK FOCUS BUT LOW ODDS

Sometimes you'll know a lot of detail about the topic you want to find online. A *specific search* is a quick way to construct a query that is tightly focused on your goal. A specific search makes use of the operator AND to join keywords together, telling the search engine to locate pages that contain *all* of the keywords. The more keywords you add, the narrower the search, and the fewer hits you are likely to get.

For example, suppose you want to locate a specific income tax form that you hope is available for downloading. A specific search query might be:

```
"income tax" AND "Form 1040" AND "Schedule B" AND download
```

Some engines have further features for performing even more specific searches. Some let you restrict matches to certain parts of a Web page, such as the page title, page text, or URL. Others let you restrict a search to particular sets of pages.

If your search is very specific, the odds are low that you'll get a hit. But if you do, it's likely to be a relevant hit, since it fits *all* your requirements (keywords). If you know a lot about your subject matter and can come up with a good set of keywords, use specific search as a first step. If the query fails, try something more general.

YOU CAN COMBINE GENERAL AND SPECIFIC SEARCH

It's perfectly fine to combine AND and OR operators to refine your search. The more OR operators you include, the more choices you allow the search engine, and the more hits you'll get. Similarly, the more AND operators you add, the more specific your query becomes, and the fewer hits you'll get.

Be aware that the meaning of your query may differ depending on how you group your keywords and operators. The following two queries have very different meanings:

```
(food OR drink) AND fun
```

```
food OR (drink AND fun)
```

The first query requires that fun be present, along with either food or drink. The second query doesn't require fun; either food can be present, or both drink and fun must be present.

In particular, be aware of what happens if you give the query:

```
food OR drink AND fun
```

with no grouping. This query will be equivalent to one of the two parenthesized queries we saw above. But which one? This issue is called *operator precedence*, and the answer depends on the search engine you use. Check your search engine's online documentation to see what it says about operator precedence. When in doubt, use parentheses (or whatever grouping method the engine supports).

Remember, AND and OR are not the only operators. See Table 5-2, "Advanced query operators," for more details.

INCREMENTAL SEARCH LETS YOU ZERO IN ON A TOPIC

"If your query doesn't produce good results, change it and try again." This common sense advice is the basis for the search strategy called *incremental search*. Incremental search allows you to narrow and broaden your search progressively until you zero in on the information you seek.

For example, suppose you want information on medical deductions for your federal income tax return. You might begin by searching with the query income tax and get 500,000 hits. Clearly you don't want to spend your day (or year) sifting through the results. What next? Modify the query slightly to make it more specific:

```
"income tax" AND deductions
```

Now you get 4,000 hits—still too many to deal with. So you try:

```
"income tax" AND deductions AND doctor
```

This time, you get no hits at all! Hmmm. Time to try modifying that doctor keyword to make it more general. How about:

```
"income tax" AND deductions AND (medical OR drugs OR hospital)
```

This time, you get 68 hits, a much more manageable number, and decide to scan them by eye.

While the idea behind incremental search is common sense, it's important to note that some search engines make it convenient to do incremental searching, while others do not. Here are some search engine features to watch for:

- *No retyping.* After a search, do you have to retype your query in order to modify it? Or does the search engine remember your last query for later editing?

- *No backtracking.* If a query doesn't return satisfactory results, do you have to press your browser's Back button to return to your old query so you can modify it? Or does the search engine conveniently redisplay your query on the search results page, ready to be edited and used in a new search?

Above all, be persistent. The information you seek may be reachable from your present query with only a small change.

How do you deal with failure?

- If my first search fails, I try a different query with the same search engine. I don't usually try the same query with a different search engine. As a last resort, I post to Usenet. —Ellie Cutler

- I try the same query with a different search engine. I put the URLs of half a dozen search engines at the top of my bookmark list to make it easy to switch search engines. —Kathleen Callaway

- I rarely get zero hits, but if they don't look right or I get only a few, I'll usually modify the query and use the same search engine. If I still couldn't find anything, my next step would depend completely on what I was searching for. Sometimes just doing things the old fashioned way—picking up the phone and asking a knowledgeable friend—will get you what you're after. —Harv Laser

- I usually try a different query with the same engine. If that failed, I would probably try some other starting points, such as checking an FAQ or asking on Usenet. —Robert Strandh

---

SUBSTRING SEARCH MATCHES SEVERAL SIMILAR KEYWORDS AT ONCE

Most search engines look for whole words. For example, if your query contains the keyword `tax`, the engine will look for `tax` but not `taxes` or `taxation`. Using general search, you can make the query:

```
tax OR taxes OR taxation
```

to get around this problem, but it's a pain to do this all the time.

Some search engines can search for partial words—called *substrings* in technical jargon—and possibly save you some work. This would allow the keyword `tax` to match `taxes` and `taxation`. The advanced query options of a search engine might allow substring searching to be turned on and off.

The main disadvantage of substring search is, like general search, it can produce many irrelevant hits. For example, searching for the substring `tax` would produce hits for irrelevant words like `taxidermist` and `syntax`.

SEARCH-AND-JUMP CAN QUICKLY NARROW A GENERAL SEARCH

When learning to use your Web browser, you may have noticed a feature that searches for text in the currently displayed Web page. The feature is usually called Find and is located in the menu or on the button bar of your browser. The Find feature examines the current Web page, locates the text you want, and automatically jumps down to the text, perhaps highlighting it for you.

The *search-and-jump* strategy makes use of the Find feature in combination with a more general search. Here's how to do it:

1. Connect to a search engine.
2. Look for a search engine option that controls the maximum number of hits displayed per page after a query. Table 5-3 explains where the setting is found on various search engines.
3. Set the number of hits per page to be the largest possible value.
4. Type your query—say, `income tax`—and start the search. When the search is over, you'll be looking at a page full of hits.
5. Now, use the Find feature to search for more specific information, for example, `Form 1040`. Find quickly searches through the hit information on the page, and if it finds a match, it scrolls the page down to the first occurrence of "Form 1040."

   Repeat this step as many times as you like.

Search-and-jump is a good strategy because it's fast. Instead of conducting multiple searches with queries, you do only one query and collect the results on one large page. Using the Find feature on that page is often faster than doing a second, more specific search with another query.

Search-and-jump has disadvantages too. By setting the maximum number of hits to be large, your initial query search might take longer than usual because a lot of hit information has to be downloaded to your computer. In addition, Find searches only for simple

Search Engine	What to Do
HotBot	Look for the number of results to return.
Lycos	Select the Custom Search link and look for Display Options.
WebCrawler	Look for the number of results to display.
Yahoo	Select the Options link and look for "matches per page."

TABLE 5-3

Setting the number of hits per page

text, so it is not as powerful as the query mechanism with keywords and operators. Finally, Find examines only the text of the hits, which is usually a summarized version of the pages themselves (e.g., the page titles and the first few lines). Even so, search-and-jump is a valuable addition to your bag of search tricks, since it gives you a way to navigate a large page full of hits.

At press time, AltaVista, Excite, InfoSeek, Magellan, and Open Text are preset to display 10 hits per page, so they aren't the best choice for the search-and-jump strategy. Search engine administrators are constantly updating their engines' capabilities, so this information is likely to change.

THE FIND FEATURE HAS OTHER INTERESTING USES

If you use a text-based Web browser, such as lynx, its Find feature can save you time. Instead of scrolling through page after page, looking for a link to select, use the Find feature to jump ahead quickly to a link.

This technique is particularly helpful on Web pages you visit frequently so you know their layout. If you know there's a link labeled Shazam far down on a long page, don't scroll to it manually. Instead, use Find to search for Shazam. If the link is the only "Shazam" on the page, you'll jump to it instantly. If not, then you can reach it in a few quick jumps.

If you use a graphics-based browser, this technique may also be useful, especially on large pages. By searching for a link that isn't currently displayed in the browser, you can save the trouble of scrolling downward by hand, looking for the link.

Case Study: Graphics card recommendations

- I did a Usenet search on AltaVista for `windows graphics cards`. —Ellie Cutler
- I searched the Web using AltaVista for `"Windows graphics cards" +best` and got a few hits. One page belonged to a magazine that had tested a bunch of cards. —Harv Laser
- I did a category search on Yahoo, starting at Computers and following along to Hardware, Peripherals, and Graphics Cards. This had a link to the Usenet newsgroup *comp.sys.ibm.pc.hardware.video.* I knew such a newsgroup existed, but I'd never have remembered the name. —Kathleen Callaway
- I used Lycos to search for `Matrox`, which I knew was a brand of graphics card. This led me to Matrox's Web site. —Robert Strandh

---

CATEGORY SEARCH LETS YOU FIND BY BROWSING

The administrators of some search engines (Yahoo, Lycos, and others) have conveniently organized their catalogs into categories for easy browsing. If you'd like to locate information on income tax, for example, you might start by selecting the general category Government. This leads to a menu of more specific categories, one of which is Agencies. This leads to Executive Branch, which leads to the Department of the Treasury, which finally leads to Internal Revenue Service.

This technique is called *category search*. Notice that no queries are necessary. Instead, you navigate from general categories to progressively more specific ones. If you don't find what you want, backtrack to a previous category, using the Back button, and continue searching from there. Not all Web search engines support category searching.

Category searches, in theory, are intuitive and convenient. In reality, you are at the mercy of the designer who created the categories. If the categories are laid out in a natural way for you, that's great. But notice that, in our example, the Executive Branch category had no link to the Internal Revenue Service. If a user didn't think to select the Department of the Treasury link, he or she might have given up here. Every hierarchy of categories will have pitfalls like this, no matter how well it's designed.

SEARCH-AND-RANK LISTS RELEVANT HITS FIRST

When a query yields a large number of hits, it is helpful to have the most relevant ones listed first so you needn't waste time scanning through the rest. This philosophy is the basis for the *search-and-rank* strategy.

Some search engines, when finding hits for a query, attempt to list the hits in order of relevance. Each hit is given a numeric value that indicates how relevant it is. This value is called a *rank* or *priority score*. The search engine then lists the hits in numeric order, according to their rank.

Unlike the previous search strategies we've seen, search-and-rank depends heavily on the search engine you use. Often, the user has no control over the ranking technique used by a search engine. The user's role in this search strategy, therefore, is more subtle. There are three ways to use the search-and-rank technique:

- *Select search engines with ranking schemes that fit your needs.* You can do this by experimenting a little. Invent a set of queries and try each of them with several different search engines. If one of the search engines consistently locates relevant hits and lists them first, then make it a habit to use that search engine. Conversely, if a search engine seems to present its hits in a random or useless order, take note.

- *Learn a search engine's ranking scheme, and write your queries to take advantage of it.* If you know how a search engine ranks its hits, this can help you to search more efficiently. For example, if you know that a particular search engine always tries to match your first keyword first, then the second keyword, then the third keyword, and so on, put your most important keyword first.

  To learn a search engine's ranking scheme, check the search engine's online documentation. Alternatively, you can ask; there's probably a link that lets you send email to the search engine administrator.

- *Learn how to modify the ranking scheme, if it's possible.* A small number of search engines allow the user to decide how hits should be ranked. For example, if you are looking for recent information, see if you can make the search engine present hits in chronological order, from the newest page to oldest. Some search engines even let you indicate which of your keywords is the most important one, thereby helping to eliminate irrelevant hits.

Hit-ranking is a difficult problem; it's the focus of active research at universities and corporations worldwide. The search-and-rank strategy, therefore, will probably not be consistently reliable for you. Still, there are cases where it will help.

CHOOSE THE STRATEGY THAT'S RIGHT FOR THE JOB

In the previous sections, we've discussed a number of search strategies—general search, specific search, incremental search, substring search, search-and-jump, category search, and search-and-rank. Different strategies work best in different situations, and their strengths and weaknesses are summarized in Table 5-4.

Strategy	Strengths	Weaknesses
General search	Likely to get a relevant hit.	Likely to get many irrelevant hits too.
Specific search	Hits are more likely to be relevant.	Low odds of getting a hit.
Incremental search	Zero in on your goal.	Multiple queries are time-consuming.
Substring search	Can simplify queries.	Likely to produce irrelevant hits.
Search-and-jump	Faster than multiple queries.	Download time may be longer; less powerful than multiple queries.
Category search	Logical, organized, great for browsing.	Relies on the skill of the organizer, whose world view may or may not match yours.
Search-and-rank	Lists the most relevant hits first.	Effective ranking functions are still undiscovered.

TABLE 5-4
General search strategies

GOPHER SEARCH WORKS MUCH THE SAME WAY

Gopher sites and FTP sites contain large collections of information not catalogued by Web search engines. Gopher sites can be searched in a manner similar to Web search engines, using keywords, operators, and the techniques we've discussed in this chapter. (FTP searching is covered in Chapter 9 when we discuss Archie.)

If you can't locate what you want on the Web, consider using Gopher search, especially if you are looking for:

- Academic papers or other university-related or scholarly information
- Press releases
- Newspaper articles

The major types of Gopher search engines are called *Jughead servers* and *Veronica servers*. Note that there isn't just one Veronica or Jughead. There are many, and they all search for Gopher information. Jughead and Veronica differ from Web search engines in the following ways:

- They search Gopher sites only.
- To get a hit, they check only the *titles* of Gopher menus, not the text inside documents. This makes them significantly weaker than Web search engines.
- A Veronica search looks through Gopher menus at thousands of Internet sites, much like a traditional Web search engine.
- A Jughead search looks through a limited set of menus, usually at a single Gopher site, much like a search engine on a specialized Web page.

Jughead and Veronica usage is very similar to that of Web search engines—just connect and try them out. You can find Jughead and Veronica servers, along with instructions for using them, at:

gopher://gopher.utah.edu

gopher://veronica.scs.unr.edu

http://www.yahoo.com/Computers_and_Internet/Internet/Gopher/Searching/

QUIZ: Web searching techniques

1. Connect to your favorite search engine. Can you determine whether it uses the active, passive, or meta-search method to locate Web pages?

2. Connect to a search engine that permits advanced search with AND and OR operators. Look up the search engine's rules of operator precedence. If you give the query food OR drink AND fun, which operator gets checked first?

3. Which operators from Table 5-2 are supported by your search engine of choice?

4. Need a vacation? Use simple queries to locate information on a desirable vacation spot. Try it with several search engines and see which yields the most relevant information.

5. Have you or a friend had a recent illness? Search the Web to locate information on it. First try it with a simple query. Then try category search on both Yahoo (*http://www.yahoo.com*) and Lycos (*http://www.lycos.com*). Which method was quicker?

6. Does your local congressional representative have a home page on the Web? Use a search engine to find out.

7. Does your favorite search engine allow you to do incremental search conveniently, without continually pressing the Back button or retyping your query?

8. An *all-in-one search page* provides access to many search engines from a single Web page. For example, it could have separate fill-in-the-blanks forms for Yahoo, AltaVista, Lycos, WebCrawler, and Excite, all on the same page. Check out some all-in-one search pages by visiting:

   *http://www.yahoo.com/Computers_and_Internet/Internet/
   World_Wide_Web/Searching_the_Web/All_in_One_Search_Pages/*

9. How do all-in-one search pages compare to meta-search engines? In what ways are they similar or different?

10. Connect to:

    gopher://veronica.scs.unr.edu/11/veronica

    and try a Veronica search for Einstein AND relativity.

Finding Places

6

This chapter digs into the low-level details about finding things on the Net. Most of the time, you won't need this level of detail, but occasionally it can save you time and effort.

This chapter covers:

- *Computer names*: they're not just random words and dots.
- *Internet domains*: how computer names are organized.
- *Finding computer and domain names*: looking them up or making educated guesses.
- *Locating computers*: finding out where in the world, or where on the Net, a computer lives.

ON THE INTERNET, "PLACES" ARE COMPUTERS

Most of the time, you needn't care where things are physically located on the Internet. Thanks to the World Wide Web, computer locations are hidden behind a point-and-click interface as pages around the world are automatically routed to your screen.

Sometimes, however, you can speed up a search by using a little knowledge about locations on the Net. If you understand the meaning of computer names, for example, you can often tell where a computer is located. This information may help you connect to online resources directly, without having to search.

If you are already familiar with computer and domain names and their use in URLs, feel free to skip ahead to the section "Guessing a computer name can save time."

EVERY INTERNET COMPUTER HAS A UNIQUE NAME

Internet computers, like users, all have names, and each name must be unique on the entire Internet. Computer names look like words separated by dots (periods). For example:

rtfm.mit.edu

www.altavista.digital.com

ftp.funet.fi

When you read a computer name out loud, say the word "dot." So, for example, the computer name *compuserve.com* is pronounced "CompuServe dot com."

Computer names have many uses. Most commonly, they are found in Internet email addresses. When you send email to your friend *steve@hahn.carnahan.com*, for example, the address indicates that the user *steve* receives email on the computer *hahn.carnahan.com*.

MANY URLS CONTAIN A COMPUTER NAME

URLs for Web pages, Gopher menus, and FTP sites contain the name of the computer where their data are stored. For example, if you connect your Web browser to the URL:

http://benson.noland.com/~marc/levine.html

this Web page is stored on the computer *benson.noland.com*. The computer name begins after the double-slash, //, and continues to the next slash or the end of the URL, whichever comes first. Here are more examples of computer names within URLs:

http://www.yahoo.com/index.html	*(www.yahoo.com)*
http://www.yahoo.com	*(www.yahoo.com)*
ftp://rtfm.mit.edu/pub/usenet/	*(rtfm.mit.edu)*
gopher://ashpool.micro.umn.edu	*(ashpool.micro.umn.edu)*

You might have noticed that the computer names of many Web sites begin with *www*, like *www.yahoo.com*. Likewise, many FTP site names begin with *ftp* and Gopher site names begin with *gopher*. This naming convention is an informal tradition, but it is not required. Computer names may vary widely. This tradition, however, will help us later when we discuss how to guess the names of computers.

THE INTERNET IS SEPARATED INTO DOMAINS

Computer names aren't just random words and dots; they have meanings. To understand them, we have to discuss Internet domains.

With hundreds of thousands of computers on the Internet, it's important to keep things organized. To do this, the Internet is separated into *domains*, which are "areas" of the Net devoted to certain purposes or organizations. These "areas" aren't physical places—they are just a helpful way to group things. For example, there is a domain for commercial businesses called *com*, a domain for colleges and universities called *edu*, and so on. These very general domains are called *top-level domains* and are listed below.

com	Commercial (for profit) organization
edu	Educational institution

gov	Government organization (non-military)
mil	Military organization
net	Networking organization
nato	NATO organization
org	Non-profit or not-for-profit organization

More country codes can be found at *http://www.ics.uci.edu/WebSoft/wwwstat/country-codes.txt.*

The top-level domains focus on the United States of America. Computers in other countries are usually in other domains, organized by country. The names of these domains are called *country codes*: *ca* for Canada, *de* for Germany (*Deutschland*), *jp* for Japan, and so on. Table 6-1 lists many country codes.

af	Afghanistan	*ir*	Iran
aq	Antarctica	*is*	Iceland
at	Austria	*it*	Italy
au	Australia	*jp*	Japan
be	Belgium	*kr*	Korea
bg	Bulgaria	*mx*	Mexico
br	Brazil	*nl*	Netherlands
ca	Canada	*no*	Norway
ch	Switzerland	*nz*	New Zealand
cl	Chile	*pe*	Peru
de	Germany	*ph*	Philippines
eg	Egypt	*pr*	Puerto Rico
es	Spain	*pt*	Portugal
fi	Finland	*ru*	Russian Federation
fr	France	*se*	Sweden
gr	Greece	*sg*	Singapore
hu	Hungary	*th*	Thailand
ie	Ireland	*tr*	Turkey
il	Israel	*uk*	United Kingdom
in	India	*us*	United States
iq	Iraq	*za*	South Africa

TABLE 6-1
Sample country codes

It's not important to memorize lots of country codes, but if you remember your own and those of a few nearby countries, you'll know whether a given computer is nearby or not, just by looking at its name.

DOMAINS CONTAIN SUBDOMAINS

Top-level domains and country codes are not sufficient for organizing the world's computers. It would be inconvenient and disorganized if every corporate computer, for example, were lumped into a single domain with no finer way to distinguish them. There are just too many computers to keep track of. So domains consist of *subdomains*, and subdomains consist of smaller subdomains, and so on. For example, the top-level *com* (commercial organization) domain consists of subdomains for different companies, such as *aol* for America Online, *time* for *Time* magazine, and *hp* for Hewlett-Packard. These subdomains define the domains *aol.com*, *time.com*, and *hp.com*, respectively.

Likewise, a subdomain can contain further, more specific subdomains. For example, the *hp* subdomain could have subdomains for its departments, such as *sales* for sales (*sales.hp.com* domain), *tech* for technical support (*tech.hp.com* domain), and *research* for research and development (*research.hp.com* domain).

In any computer name, each word represents a subdomain, and each suffix represents a domain. For example, in the computer name *www.yahoo.com*, the subdomains (words) are *www*, *yahoo*, and *com*, and the domain names (suffixes) are *www.yahoo.com*, *yahoo.com*, and *com*. The *www.yahoo.com* domain contains a single computer (the Yahoo web site), the *yahoo.com* domain contains all Yahoo-related computers, and the *com* domain contains all corporate computers.

You may have noticed that the top-level domain, *com*, is both a domain and a subdomain. This is because *com* is both a word and a suffix; the same is true of any other top-level domain or country code. (This isn't important to remember.)

Alternic
http://www.alternic.net
Additional top-level domain names have been proposed; see this site for more information.

COMPUTER NAMES ARE BEST UNDERSTOOD FROM RIGHT TO LEFT

Now that you've seen subdomains, computer names should look less cryptic. In particular, a name gets more specific as you read its subdomains from right to left. For example, the subdomains of the computer name *rtfm.mit.edu* mean:

edu   On the Internet, there are educational institutions.

mit   Inside the *edu* domain, there's the Massachusetts Institute of Technology.

rtfm   Inside the *mit.edu* domain, there's a computer called *rtfm*.

The subdomains of *www.altavista.digital.com* mean:

com   On the Internet, there are commercial businesses.

digital   Inside the *com* domain, there's Digital Equipment Corporation.

altavista   Inside the *digital.com* domain, there's the AltaVista search engine project.

www   Inside the *altavista.digital.com* domain, there's a computer called *www*.

COMPUTER NAMES MAY HAVE DIFFERENT NUMBERS OF SUBDOMAINS

Some of our example computer names have three subdomains separated by dots, and some have four. In fact, computer names can consist of two subdomains, or five, or even more. The reason is beyond the scope of this book, but it's perfectly normal, and the rule is still the same: the computer name gets more specific as you read from right to left. Figure 6-1 shows how domains are "nested" inside one another.

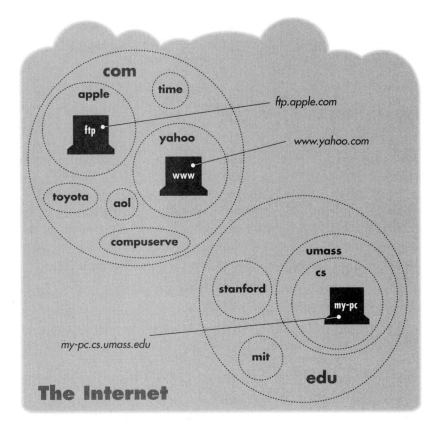

com
apple
time
ftp.apple.com
ftp
yahoo
www.yahoo.com
www
toyota
aol
compuserve
umass
cs
stanford
my-pc
my-pc.cs.umass.edu
mit
edu

The Internet

FIGURE 6-1
*Domains are nested
inside each other*

GUESSING A COMPUTER NAME CAN SAVE TIME

Suppose that your brother-in-law works at the company Widgets Inc., and you want to locate its Web page. You don't know anything about the company except the name, so you connect to your favorite Web search engine and try the simple query widgets inc. In response, you get 158 hits. Apparently, lots of companies make widgets, and even more have "Inc" in their names. Thankfully, one of the hits is correct, and you locate the page after only 10 minutes of wading through irrelevant hits. The URL turns out to be:

http://www.widgets.com

Hmm…What a plain-looking URL. It begins with the required *http://* and ends with a computer name, *www.widgets.com*, containing the name of the company. Since many Web computer names begin with *www*, and company domain names invariably end with *com*, you might find yourself thinking, "I could have guessed that URL in less time than it took to search."

You're right. The next few sections explain how to make educated guesses about domain names. From there, one can make educated guesses about URLs.

DOMAIN NAMES OFTEN FOLLOW PATTERNS

When guessing a computer name, first try to guess the last two words of the name. The last two words are informally called "the domain name" of the computer. In the previous example, the domain name, *widgets.com*, isn't difficult to guess because it's just the company name followed by the required *com*. Some domain names indeed use the full name of the organization, but many do not. Here are some of the more common patterns for domain names.

- *Full name.* For example, Stanford University's domain name is *stanford.edu*, and Prodigy's is *prodigy.com*.

- *Acronym.* For example, The Johns Hopkins University's domain name is *jhu.edu*, and America Online uses *aol.com*.

- *Abbreviation.* For example, the domain name of State University College at Buffalo is *snybuf.edu*, and Gateway 2000 uses *gw2k.com*. As you might suspect, abbreviations can be difficult to guess.

- *Products.* For example, when the movie *Independence Day* was released in 1996, Twentieth Century Fox created a new Internet domain, *id4.com,* to promote the movie. (Their regular domain is *foxhome.com.*)

If you're guessing a domain name, which pattern should you try? There's no way to know in advance, but with practice, you'll develop a feel for it. Guessing doesn't always work, of course. I recently tried to locate the National Science Foundation and guessed *nsf.org*. Instead of finding the NSF, I found a lengthy document about drinking water. (The correct domain is *nsf.gov*.)

URLS CAN BE GUESSED FROM DOMAIN NAMES

Here's a short recipe for turning a domain name into a likely URL where interesting things (Web pages, FTP archives, etc.) can be found:

1. Discover the domain name by guessing or other means.

2. Put *www* and a dot in front of the domain name.

3. Depending on which service you want—Web, FTP, or Gopher— add the required URL part:

   ▪ For a Web site, add *http://* to the beginning.

   ▪ For an FTP site, add *ftp://* to the beginning.

   ▪ For a Gopher site, add *gopher://* to the beginning.

4. Use your Web browser to connect directly to the URL.

This recipe doesn't always work, but when it does, it's faster than doing a formal search. Table 6-2 gives examples of guessing a Web page URL from a domain name.

Organization	Domain name	Guessed Web page URL
American Red Cross	*redcross.org*	*http://www.redcross.org*
Boston College	*bc.edu*	*http://www.bc.edu*
Time Magazine	*time.com*	*http://www.time.com*
The White House	*whitehouse.gov*	*http://www.whitehouse.gov*

TABLE 6-2
Choosing a likely URL

ACADEMIC DEPARTMENT DOMAINS CAN OFTEN BE GUESSED

Colleges and universities tend to create subdomains for their departments. These subdomain names are usually abbreviations of the department name, though sometimes (rarely) the whole name is used. Table 6-3 shows some common abbreviations.

Once you have guessed a domain name, the main Web pages of colleges and universities can often be located by guessing, completely avoiding a Web search. For instance, if the domain name is:

mycollege.edu

add *www* at the beginning, to get the name of the Web site computer:

www.mycollege.edu

Finally, add the required beginning of any Web page URL:

http://www.mycollege.edu

and you have a very good guess for the main Web page. To guess the Web page for a department, put the department name after the *www*:

http://www.chem.mycollege.edu

and give it a try. As mentioned earlier, Web site computer names needn't begin with *www*, so another reasonable guess is:

http://chem.mycollege.edu

Subject	Common Abbreviations
Art History	*art, arth, arthist*
Astronomy	*astro, phast*
Biology	*bio, biol*
Biochemistry	*bio, biochem*
Chemistry	*chem*
Chemical Engineering	*che*
Computer Science	*cs, cis, cse, cmpsci*
Electrical Engineering	*ee, eecs, ecs, cse, eecs*
English	*eng, engl*
Geology	*geo, geol*
History	*hist*
Legal Studies	*legal, law*
Materials Science	*mse*
Mathematics	*math*
Physics	*phy, phys*
Political Science	*polsci*
Psychology	*psy, psych, sbs*
Sociology	*soc*

TABLE 6-3

Common academic abbreviations

Where's Usenet?

Where is Usenet located? Unlike Web pages, FTP sites, and other Internet resources that have a clear location (the computer that stores them), Usenet doesn't exist in a single place.

When an article is posted to Usenet, it does not have a single destination. Rather, thousands of copies of the article are broadcast worldwide to computers configured to receive Usenet news. When you read a Usenet news article, you're reading one of those copies.

Usenet is similar to a published magazine. Electronic copies of the magazine are distributed to thousands of computers where the articles can be read. Unlike a magazine, however, the publisher isn't located in one place. Instead, every Usenet reader can publish (post) articles.

Because Usenet has no central location, newsgroup URLs don't contain a computer name, just the name of the newsgroup, as in:

news:rec.music.classical

WATCH FOR THE MISSING *HTTP*

Many companies include their Web addresses in advertisements, but some abbreviate the URL. For instance, an advertisement might list only *www.company.com* as the address of a Web page. The company has omitted the first part of the URL, *http://*, to save space. The full URL is:

http://www.company.com

Some browsers, notably Netscape Navigator, allow the *http://* part of a URL to be omitted. If you ask to connect to *www.company.com*, the browser will assume you mean *http://www.company.com* and connect to that page. This is a handy shortcut. Other browsers do not allow this omission, however, so users must add the *http://* before connecting.

Netscape Navigator version 3.0 (or higher) will also let you omit other parts of the URL. In our above example, if you ask to connect to *company*, the browser will automatically assume you mean *http://www.company.com* and make the connection. Currently, the domain *com* is always assumed; this shortcut won't work for *edu*, *org*, or other top-level domains. If you ask to connect to *harvard*, for example, Netscape Navigator assumes you want the *harvard.com* domain, instead of *harvard.edu*. Expect to see this URL-guessing feature greatly expanded in future browsers.

GUESSING WON'T ALWAYS WORK

Some organizations choose domain names that are not similar to their real names. This can happen for various reasons:

- The organization does not have its own domain, but borrows or buys space in another domain. This is common in online "shopping malls" that represent multiple businesses in a single domain.
- The organization is owned by a parent organization, and the parent's name is used as the domain name.
- All of the natural-sounding domain names for the organization were already being used by other organizations.
- The organization wants to be different.

As a result, these organizations' domain names are difficult to guess. A Web search for the organization's name would fare better.

Sometimes a reasonable guess can be wildly wrong. I once needed to find the Web page for Gateway 2000, a computer vendor, so naturally I tried *http://www.gateway.com*. To my surprise, *gateway.com* turned out to be the domain of a completely unrelated consulting company. The funny part is that many other people had made the same mistake—so many that *gateway.com* put a notice on its Web page about it, with a link to Gateway 2000's Web page at *http://www.gw2k.com*. So one wrong guess unexpectedly led to a shortcut.

THE INTERNIC CAN REVEAL DOMAIN NAMES

The InterNIC is a registry for domain names on the Internet. The InterNIC's *whois database* (pronounced "who is") keeps track of the domain names in most of the top-level domains (*com*, *edu*, *org*, etc.). Their Web page at:

http://www.internic.net/wp/whois.html

permits searching for domain names by keyword.

Why not try the InterNIC right away, instead of guessing? You certainly may, but in my experience, querying the InterNIC is not much faster than doing a Web search. My own method is to guess first, try the InterNIC second, and do a Web search if those methods fail.

The InterNIC does not cover domains that end in country codes. There's no central authority that does. Each country may (or may not) have a whois service available for querying. Some whois services are listed at:

http://www.yahoo.com/Computers_and_Internet/Internet/
Domain_Registration/

and in Appendix A. The InterNIC is discussed in more detail in Chapter 7.

EVERY INTERNET COMPUTER HAS TWO LOCATIONS

Each Internet computer has a *geographical* location: where it physically sits in the world. It also has a *network* location: its position on the Internet in relation to other computers. When you are interacting with a remote computer, the distance can be measured according to either location.

Ordinary geographic distance, measured in miles or kilometers, may affect the speed of transmission between computers. So if the information you seek can be found on two different computers—one in Washington, D.C., and the other in Australia—it makes sense to choose the location that's closer to you, since the transmission may be faster. The InterNIC and other whois services tell you the geographic location of a domain when you make a query; you may also guess it from the domain name.

Network distance, measured in *hops*, also affects the speed of transmission between computers. One hop is a transmission from one computer to another. Digital information, such as an email message or a Web page request, typically travels through a series of computers before reaching its destination. Each computer-to-computer transmission is another hop, as in Figure 6-2. Each hop takes time, and if a computer or connection in the chain is slow, the information is delayed further.

Geographic distance and network distance needn't be related. A computer 1,000 miles away could be closer to you, in hops, than one in a neighboring town, depending on how the networks are set up. So while geographic distance is reasonable for estimating transmission time, it's not always reliable. In addition, distance is not the only

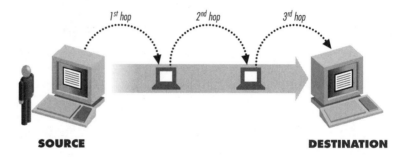

FIGURE 6-2

*Computer data travel-
ing through a network*

factor that affects transmission speed. Network load—how busy the network is, handling data requests from large numbers of people—can also slow down transmission.

By the way, busy or faraway Web sites are sometimes duplicated in several geographic areas to provide more efficient access for people in different regions of the world. These duplicates are called *mirror sites* or just *mirrors*. You may see this term used on Web pages devoted to downloading files, especially freely distributable software.

THE TRACEROUTE PROGRAM MEASURES NETWORK DISTANCE

You can't reliably guess network distance from a domain name. If you're curious to know how many hops are between your computer and a remote computer, there are ways to find out. Most of the time, you don't need this information. If you are transferring large files, however, or need to contact a site repeatedly, it makes sense to choose a site that is only a small number of hops away. This can save you time and help lighten your load on the network.

The traceroute program is designed to count and to time the hops between computers. Originally available on UNIX computers, it now comes standard with Windows 95, where it's called tracert.exe. A similar, freely distributable program called HopCheck is also available for Windows. For Macintosh, try WhatRoute or MacTraceroute, both freely distributable. (Freely distributable software can be located using the methods of Chapter 9.)

The program outputs a list of computers that lie between you and a remote computer you specify. The number of hops is the number of computers minus one: two computers means one hop, ten computers means nine hops, etc. You might be surprised to find that computers you regularly contact are 15 or 20 hops away.

If you cannot get your hands on a traceroute program, some Web sites offer a similar service. However, they display the number of hops from a remote computer to *themselves*, not to you. Still, they can show you what traceroute looks like. To locate such a Web page, do a Web search for traceroute. At press time, one is located at:

http://www.aloha.com/traceroute.html

Again, traceroute is rarely needed, but it is occasionally helpful if you're doing a lot of file transfers or if you encounter a slowdown in the network and want to see which hops are taking the most time. It can also be educational and fun to see the path followed by your data.

---

1. Can you guess the domain names of the following?

   (a) Apple Computers

   (b) Warner Brothers Records

   (c) Swarthmore College

   (d) Rochester Institute of Technology

   Check your answers at the InterNIC.

2. Can you guess the URL of the home page of the following?

   (a) Microsoft

   (b) The Stanford University computer science department

   (c) The Federal Bureau of Investigation

   (d) Tower Records

   (e) Greenpeace

   Check your answers with a Web browser.

3. Choose a country from the list of country codes. Using Web search techniques, try to find a whois service, like the InterNIC's, for that country.

4. Pick your two favorite Web search engines. Use a traceroute-like program to determine which one is closer to your computer, in hops. Then query the InterNIC to find out where the search engines are located geographically.

5. Pick an Internet computer that you think is close to you. Use traceroute to see how many hops away it is. You might be surprised!

QUIZ: Finding places

Finding People

7

If you want to locate someone—a colleague, a seminar speaker, a long-lost friend—the Internet has numerous resources to help you search. You can even locate people who don't use the Internet. In this chapter, we'll discuss strategies for finding people:

- *Web resources*: search engines, "white pages" directories, InterNIC directories, and telephone directories.

- *Usenet resources*: newsgroups and Usenet search engines.

- *Local resources*: those available from your online service provider.

- *Guesses*: turning a hunch into success.

As a running example, we'll search for "Frances Factfinder," an imaginary person.

This chapter is different from the others because it relies heavily on the particular search facilities available. They are all poor substitutes for a single, global directory of users, but they're the best we have right now.

BE SOCIALLY RESPONSIBLE

Before you start using the Net to find people, it's worth mentioning that some people don't *want* to be contacted, so they do not publicize their addresses. If someone does not want to receive your email, please be respectful and leave the person alone. This rule applies especially to advertisers who gather email messages and broadcast "junk email" to thousands or millions of users.

Similarly, it's considered impolite to publicize an unpublicized email address. It's just like spreading around an unlisted phone number. Please respect other people's privacy just as you would like them to respect yours.

DON'T FORGET THE TELEPHONE

The quickest way to locate somebody's email address or Web page is sometimes so simple that people don't think of it. Just call the person on the phone and ask. If you don't know the phone number, call Information. The few pennies you'll spend on a long-distance call might be cheaper than spending your valuable time searching.

WEB SEARCH ENGINES CAN LOCATE PEOPLE'S HOME PAGES

If you want to find somebody on the Net, your first attempt might be to search for his or her home page, if it exists. To search for Frances Factfinder's home page, for example, you could connect to a Web search engine and type the simple query:

```
Frances Factfinder
```

While this may work, some problems can arise. For instance, Frances might call herself "Fran" or "Frannie" on her home page. You can avoid problems with nicknames by using an advanced query, as we discussed in Chapter 5:

```
(Fran OR Frances OR Frannie) AND Factfinder
```

(Remember that you'll have to use the advanced query language supported by your search engine of choice, which might use operators other than AND, OR, and parentheses.)

Another potential problem is that the query `Frances Factfinder` may unintentionally match Web pages that happen to contain the keywords `Frances` and `Factfinder,` but not necessarily next to each other. If some random page contains the names Frances Smith and Gary Factfinder, for example, your query might match it. You may need to use the search engine's advanced query language to indicate that the keywords `Frances` and `Factfinder` must be adjacent to match the query. Some search engines use double quotes for this purpose:

```
"Fran Factfinder" OR "Frances Factfinder" OR "Frannie
Factfinder"
```

Even if you take these precautions, your query may find many people named Frances Factfinder on the Internet. Consider making your query more specific, adding information (with AND) that is likely to be on her home page, such as the name of her home town or a school she attended:

```
"Frances Factfinder" AND Boston AND "Hackerville High
School"
```

Many people don't have home pages, so you might think this kind of search has a low chance of success. However, these queries can match not only a home page, but also any mention of Frances Factfinder on other people's Web pages. Such a match will at least point you toward somebody who knows Frances, and you could send email to him or her for more information.

"WHITE PAGES" ARE DIRECTORIES OF EMAIL ADDRESSES

Although there is no central directory of users on the Internet, some people and companies have created directories and made them available on the Web. Like the Web search engines we saw in Chapter 5, these electronic "white pages" can be passive, requiring users to register themselves, or active, seeking out users' email addresses automatically (often from Usenet news articles).

At press time, the best white pages directory is `Four11` (pronounced "four eleven"), available for free at:

http://www.four11.com

**soc.net-people
Email FAQs**

http://www.qucis.queensu. ca/FAQs/email/finding.html for general information.

http://www.qucis.queensu. ca/FAQs/email/college.html for college addresses.

This Usenet newsgroup has FAQs for locating people's email addresses.

Four11 allows you to look up users' email addresses and home pages by entering their name and other personal information: geographic location, high school attended, hobbies, and other interesting criteria.

Some other large white pages directories are the OKRA net.citizen Directory Service, located at:

http://okra.ucr.edu/okra/

and the Internet Address Finder, located at:

http://www.iaf.net

It's hard for Internet white pages to stay up to date, since email addresses change frequently. Don't be surprised if a listed email address is no longer valid. (One white pages service had 15 of my old, obsolete email addresses in their database, plus two correct ones. I deleted the obsolete addresses using the page's Remove Address link.)

Some companies and universities make available their employee and/or student databases on the Web. If you suspect that Frances Factfinder works for Hackerworks Inc., for example, try locating their Web site and looking for a personnel database.

To find other white page services, try giving the query white pages to a Web search engine.

Case Study: Find a long-lost friend.

- I tried *www.four11.com* but couldn't find my friend. So I did a simple search in AltaVista on her name, in quotes, and I got three hits. Two of them couldn't have been her, but the third was a possibility. —Fern Dickman

- I went to Yahoo and used their People Search page. —Kathleen Callaway

- If I had access to America Online, I'd try searching its member directory. I might also try a Usenet search engine. —Ellie Cutler

- I've tried using various search engines and often failed. The problem with people's names is there's too much duplication. You don't know if you're hitting the right person or not, unless you're looking for a unique name like Aloysius F. Snodgrass III. I had a friend in high school named Rick Nelson, but there are plenty of Rick Nelsons on the Net. This is one kind of search I'd probably approach in an old-fashioned way. I'd try to locate his parents' home, probably in the same neighborhood he used to live in, and call them. Or I'd try the high school office of records, or the organizer of the high school reunion. —Harv Laser

TRY THE INTERNIC'S X.500 AND WHOIS SERVICES

The InterNIC (Chapter 6) maintains two searchable databases of Internet users. The more generally useful one is the X.500 directory service, available at:

http://www.internic.net/wp/x500.html

X.500 is a "distributed" directory, created by organizations around the world and linked together via the Internet. The InterNIC allows you to browse the directories in search of somebody, as long as you have a general idea of where in the world the person is located.

The InterNIC's X.500 Web service guides you through several menus of choices as you search. For instance, if Frances Factfinder were a professor at MIT, you would first select USA, followed by Massachusetts, followed by Massachusetts Institute of Technology. From there, you could search MIT's X.500 directory to locate Frances's email address.

Not all organizations participate in the X.500 directory service. For instance, if MIT had not created an X.500 directory and registered it with the InterNIC, you wouldn't be able to find Frances Factfinder by this means.

The InterNIC also administers the *whois* database (Chapter 6), one of the oldest databases of Internet users. It's available for searching at:

http://www.internic.net/wp/whois.html

but it's not a general-purpose user database. It primarily lists the administrators of Internet computer systems. (In the early days of the Internet, these folks made up a significant portion of the Net population!)

If the InterNIC has moved its Web pages and the above URLs have changed, try connecting to:

http://www.internic.net

and browsing to find the directories' new locations.

ADDRESS AND TELEPHONE
DATABASES ARE AVAILABLE

If you know a person's name and want to find his or her address and telephone number, this is possible on the Web even if the person doesn't use the Internet. Services like Switchboard, available at:

http://www.switchboard.com

and Who Where, available at:

http://www.whowhere.com

allow this kind of searching, even if you know only part of a person's name. For instance, you could search for the last name Factfinder in the entire United States or just in Arkansas.

Some directories can search for a person by phone number—that is, you enter the phone number, and the search engine tells you whose number it is. Due to privacy concerns, these directories come and go. At press time, one is located at:

http://www.pc.411.com

To locate others, try a web search for "reverse telephone".

Finally, several companies sell CD-ROM discs containing large telephone databases. If you're interested, ask your local software retailer for more information.

HELP OTHER PEOPLE
FIND YOU

It's fun to receive email from somebody you haven't heard from in a long time. If you'd like other people to find you on the Net, consider registering your name, email address, and home page URL with an Internet white pages service. Most white pages have a "Register" link on their main page. You might want to register with several white pages, since you don't know which ones will be used by people when looking for you.

Before you register, however, find out the service's privacy policy. (Often, a link on the main page leads to this information.) In particular, look for a service that discourages or forbids marketers to use the database for commercial purposes, such as junk mailings.

I desperately needed to locate a colleague who was out of the country, attending a conference in Scotland. Nobody knew how to locate him, so I decided to try searching the Net.

Case Study: Be persistent!

I knew a few words of the conference name, so I used them as keywords and did a Web search. Success—there was a hit. But the hit was obsolete; the Web page had moved. Fortunately, the sponsor had been thoughtful and left a forwarding link, which I followed to the computer science department of the university hosting the conference. Their home page had a Conferences link, but when I selected it, my colleague's conference wasn't listed. I was stuck.

Searching for clues, I examined the obsolete URL. It contained the word *susan*, implying that the old page may have belonged to someone named Susan. I went back to the computer science department page and looked for a Susan on the faculty. There was exactly one. I followed a link to her home page, saw a Research link, and selected it. This led to a page with a link for the conference!

The conference page had a link to hotel information for the attendees. The hotel page had a phone number. Two minutes later, I was speaking with my colleague on the phone.

When registering, be cautious how much information you reveal about yourself. Remember that anybody in the world could read your listing. Generally, it's safe to register your email address, but I do not recommend registering your home address or phone number.

Finally, remember to update your listing when you change email addresses.

USENET SEARCH ENGINES CAN LOCATE EMAIL ADDRESSES

Many people don't realize that Usenet search engines can be very effective for locating people. (We introduced Usenet search engines in Chapter 4.) Articles posted to Usenet contain the author's email address and possibly full name. Thus, if you search through collections of old Usenet articles, you might locate the name of the person you seek, and hence his or her email address.

For example, suppose Frances Factfinder posted a note in *rec.arts.po-ems* last year. If you connect to Deja News:

http://www.dejanews.com

and search for `Frances Factfinder`, Deja News will locate and display her article and her email address.

As we discussed in Chapter 4, Deja News and AltaVista are currently the reigning Usenet search engines. One other Usenet search engine, however, is specially tailored for locating email addresses. It's called the Usenet Addresses Service, located at:

http://usenet-addresses.mit.edu

and it allows you to search its database of millions of email addresses culled from Usenet postings over the years.

FIND LOCAL USERS VIA YOUR ONLINE SERVICE PROVIDER

Your online service provider may allow you to locate other users of the same service. Here's how to do it for several major online service providers and on UNIX machines.

- *America Online*: Use keyword `member directory`, then choose Search The Member Directory.
- *CompuServe:* `GO DIRECTORY`.
- *Microsoft Network:* Run Microsoft Exchange. From the Tools menu, choose Address Book. When the address book opens, set Show Names to be Microsoft Network. Then choose Find from the Tools menu. Fill in your search criteria and click OK.
- *Prodigy*: Use the jumpword `member list`.
- *UNIX machines*: The finger program displays information about a user, given his or her username. For example, to see information about local user *factfinder*, type:

```
finger factfinder
```

Finger may be used to display information about a user on another computer. For instance, if Frances Factfinder has an account on a different machine, give her whole email address to finger:

```
finger factfinder@some.machine.net
```

Not all computers allow you to "finger" their users, however. See the section on vrfy for an alternative.

Your online service provider also might have local resources for looking up addresses and telephone numbers around the world.

FOR ADVENTUROUS USERS: VRFY

If you have computer programming experience, and you access the Internet via TCP/IP (either by direct connection, PPP, or SLIP), you can take advantage of a powerful program called vrfy. Written by Eric Wassenaar, vrfy (pronounced "verify") may succeed when finger does not. In order for a finger command like the following to succeed:

```
finger factfinder@some.machine.net
```

three things must be true:

- The computer *some.machine.net* must be directly connected to the Internet. If not, finger will respond with "unknown host."
- The user *factfinder* must have a real computer account, not just a mail alias, on *some.machine.net*. finger can't deal with mail aliases; they yield a "user unknown" error message.
- The computer *some.machine.net* must have special software installed, called a *finger daemon*, that allows other people to finger it. If not, finger will respond "connection timed out" after it tries to find the finger daemon but fails.

vrfy has none of these weaknesses. It can locate computers not directly connected to the Net, it can handle mail aliases (like *postmaster*), and it doesn't require the remote computer to run a finger daemon. How does it work? It silently queries the email software on the remote computer. Since most Internet computers run email software, vrfy usually succeeds if the desired user is known to the remote computer. Here's a command to determine whether Frances Factfinder's email address is *factfinder@some.machine.net*:

```
vrfy -e factfinder@some.machine.net
```

If the command succeeds, you'll see a response like this:

```
<factfinder@some.machine.net>
```

indicating that the email address is valid, or:

```
<factfinder@yet.another.machine.net>
```

indicating that Frances's email is forwarded to another machine (but *factfinder@some.machine.net* is fine to use). If vrfy fails, the response will look something like this:

```
factfinder@some.machine.net... User Unknown
```

Because vrfy invisibly uses email software to contact other computers, you may occasionally see a cryptic response. If you see a response that contains a vertical bar, like this:

```
<"|/usr/local/bin/myprogram">
```

it means the user's email is automatically forwarded to a computer program, and vrfy cannot trace any further. If the response contains the word majordomo or listserv, or if the response is a list of email addresses, the email address is actually a mailing list.

Most computers do not have vrfy installed, so you will probably have to download and compile the program yourself. (This is where programming experience may be needed.) You can download the source code of vrfy from several computers on the Net:

http://gatekeep.cs.utah.edu/hpux/Networking/Admin/vrfy-94.09.29/

http://hpux.ask.uni-karlsruhe.de/hpux/Networking/Admin/ vrfy-94.09.29.html

http://escher.usr.dsi.unimi.it/hpux/Networking/Admin/vrfy-94.09.29/

If none of these sites is current, do a Web search for `vrfy`, `vrfy-94.09.29`, or `Eric Wassenaar`.

GUESSING MIGHT BE FASTER THAN SEARCHING

Some users don't have home pages, don't register their email addresses with any white pages, don't post on Usenet, and aren't listed in any online databases. Even so, sometimes you can make an educated guess about someone's location on the Net. A good hunch can save a lot of search time. We'll look at two examples: guessing an email address, and guessing a home page URL.

SOMETIMES YOU CAN GUESS AN EMAIL ADDRESS

To guess a person's email address, you need to guess two pieces of information: his or her username, and the computer that has the account. You'll also need a way of testing your guess. This could be a program like finger or vrfy, described earlier, or a member directory service on your online service provider. Don't "test" your guesses by sending email to dozens of random, potential addresses, however. It's impolite.

First, try to guess the computer name, as we discussed in Chapter 6. Then try to guess the username. Usernames can be just about anything, but they often take a standard form. Table 7-1 shows common forms for usernames, assuming we are looking for Frances Q. Factfinder.

Should you try every combination, one at a time? Sometimes it comes to that. But other times you can take a shortcut if you know the username of *another* user on the *same machine*. Some system administrators insist that usernames on their machines must fit a standard format, like those shown in Table 7-1. Look at the format of the other username you know, and apply it to Frances Factfinder's name. If you don't know any other usernames on the machine, and you have access to a finger program, try fingering the machine without a username:

```
finger @some.machine.net
```

and you may see a list of the users who are logged on to that machine. If their usernames fit a standard format, then Frances's probably does too.

General Idea	Example
Last name	*factfinder*
First 8 letters of last name	*factfind*
First name	*frances*
Nickname	*fran*
First.Last	*Frances.Factfinder*
First_Last	*Frances_Factfinder*
First.Middle.Last	*Frances.Q.Factfinder*
First_Middle_Last	*Frances_Q_Factfinder*
First and last initials	*ff*
First, middle, and last initials	*fqf*
First initial, last name	*ffactfinder*
First initial, last name, 8 letters	*ffactfin*
First name, last initial	*francesf*
Last name 6 letters, first name 2 letters	*factfifr*
Last name 6 letters, 2 initials	*factfifq*

TABLE 7-1:
Standard forms of user-names

Speaking of finger, sometimes you can finger a user on another machine by first or last name:

```
finger frances@some.machine.net
```

```
finger factfinder@some.machine.net
```

Even if Frances's username is different from *frances* and *factfinder*, some finger daemons are smart enough to locate users by their real names.

EMAIL ADDRESSES CHANGE

Suppose you've been happily exchanging email with Frances Factfinder for many weeks, but one day, you receive a cryptic-looking message in return:

```
From: MAILER-DAEMON@some.machine.net
Subject: Returned mail: User unknown

— The following addresses have delivery notifications —
  factfinder@some.machine.net (unrecoverable error)

— Transcript of session follows —
  ... while talking to some.machine.net:
  >>> RCPT To:<factfinder@some.machine.net>
  <<< 550 <factfinder@some.machine.net>... User unknown
  550 factfinder@some.machine.net... User unknown
```

Notice the message "User unknown." Frances' computer account on *some.machine.net* has apparently disappeared. This happens all the time on the Net as people switch online service providers.

How can you locate Frances' new email address? The quickest way is probably to pick up the telephone and call her, but if you don't have her phone number, you can try writing to the postmaster of Frances' old online service provider. The postmaster's email address is the same as Frances' old one, but with her username (*factfinder*) replaced by *postmaster*: *postmaster@some.machine.net*. If this address fails, try mailing to the postmaster of the whole *machine.net* domain, *postmaster@machine.net*. Postmasters are busy people, so don't expect a quick answer, and remember to ask politely.

Note that a good online service provider will forward email to a user's new address, at least for a short time.

TRY GUESSING A USER'S HOME PAGE

A user's email address can sometimes be used to guess the person's home page URL. If you get good at this, it's faster than doing a Net search for the user's home page.

Suppose that Frances Factfinder's email address is *fran@hackhaven.org*. Here's how to take an educated guess at her home page URL, building a guess one step at a time.

1. A Web page URL almost always begins with:

   http://

2. Many Web sites are on computers whose names begin with *www*. So Frances's home page is conceivably on *www.hackhaven.org*. Our guess so far is:

   http://www.hackhaven.org

3. Users' home pages are often referenced by a username, preceded by a tilde character:

   http://www.hackhaven.org/~fran/

4. Use your Web browser to connect to this URL. If it exists, you have made a successful guess!

Some Web site names don't begin with *www*, and some don't require tildes in front of the username when referencing a home page. So you might also try:

> *http://www.hackhaven.org/fran/* (No ~)
>
> *http://hackhaven.org/~fran/*   (No *www*)
>
> *http://hackhaven.org/fran/*   (Neither)

Don't type these URLs individually—use your computer's cut-and-paste utilities to speed up the process.

If all of these guesses fail, try connecting to the "roots" of these URLs:

http://www.hackhaven.org

http://hackhaven.org

One of these is likely the main Web page for *hackhaven.org*, which might have links to its users' home pages.

EVEN PEOPLE WHO DON'T USE THE NET CAN BE LOCATED

If you know a few facts about a person—a past employer, an alma mater, the name of a mutual acquaintance—the Net can provide a good starting point for locating him or her, even if he or she doesn't use the Net. Rather than searching for Frances Factfinder's name, for example, search for this related information. Perhaps her old employer or school has a Web site with a contact person who can point you in the right direction. (Colleges and universities can be great starting points, especially if they have an alumni search service online.) Or perhaps one of your mutual acquaintances has a home

> A surprising way to find people is to search for genealogy resources on the Net. These often contain pointers to other resources for locating people.
>
> Genealogy is the study of tracing family histories. Try searching for `genealogy` using a Web search engine.

Genealogy resources

page. You might be surprised how many people can be located through a friend, or a friend of a friend, who happens to be on the Net.

USENET'S *SOC.NET-PEOPLE* IS A LAST RESORT

The play *Six Degrees of Separation* makes the claim that every person on Earth is connected to every other by a chain of at most six people. Given any person (say, Frances Factfinder), you know somebody who knows someone else, who knows someone else, and so on, who knows Frances. This is the philosophy behind the Usenet newsgroup *soc.net-people*. Just post a note, saying that you are looking for Frances Factfinder, and if you're lucky, one of Frances' friends will see your request and answer you.

Dan Schneider, Cary Timar, and Sridhar Venkataraman, participants in the newsgroup, suggest that in your post, you should include information about the person's most recent whereabouts, for instance, a town or a company. This increases your chances of catching the attention of someone in that location. The best way to do this is in the Subject line of your message, like this:

```
Subject: Washington DC - Frances Factfinder
```

To be a polite Net citizen, please treat *soc.net-people* as a last resort to be used only when all other methods have failed. Remember that a single post to Usenet is copied to more than 200,000 computers worldwide. Thousands of computers will devote time to processing your request, and thousands of people will spend time reading your request.

Also, don't expect tremendous results from *soc.net-people*. Most people on the Net don't read this newsgroup and therefore won't see your request, and it's frequently cluttered with off-topic articles. But

QUIZ: Finding people

1. Perform Web searches to locate anything you can on the following people:

   (a) A former classmate

   (b) The author of a favorite book

   (c) Your doctor

   (d) Your next-door neighbor

   (e) Your parents and/or children

   (f) Yourself

2. Locate an Internet telephone directory other than the ones mentioned in this chapter. Look up a friend you haven't seen in a long time.

3. Does the telephone directory you found in question 2 have any useful features the other directories lack?

4. Look yourself up in various white pages and telephone directories on the Net. If there's no listing for you, consider adding one. If there's an incorrect listing, delete it.

5. Locate the email address of your employer or your professor. Then use Deja News to locate Usenet articles he or she has written.

6. Use a Web search engine to locate a genealogy resource. Can you find information about your own family history?

you might get lucky. At the very least, the newsgroup's FAQ is worth reading for its tips on locating people.

Finding Kindred Spirits

8

No matter what your interests are, somebody else on the Internet shares them. Whether you love baseball or business, sushi or sky-diving, Rachmaninoff or rap music, somewhere on the Net there's a community waiting to welcome you. In the physical world, it can be hard to meet people who share your favorite activities or pastimes. On the Internet, locating such people is much easier... if you know where to look.

Some people speak of "the Internet community," as if every user were part of the same clan. These days, the Net population is too large to be a single, cohesive group. While all users share at least one interest (the Internet itself), it's more accurate to say that the Net consists of many communities. This chapter will help you find one—or several—that match your interests. We'll discuss:

- *Mailing lists*, for semi-private discussions among a known group of people.

- *Newsgroups*, for open, public discussions.

- *Chat groups*, for real-time discussions, public or private.

MAILING LISTS ARE SEMI-PRIVATE DISCUSSION GROUPS

Mailing lists are one of the premier ways that groups communicate and socialize on the Internet. Using ordinary email, a mailing list lets you carry on conversations with a group. Mailing lists are great for meeting people who share an interest.

Thousands of mailing lists exist on the Internet today. Each one is devoted to a particular topic, and topics are pretty diverse. For instance, there are Internet mailing lists for discussing finance, chocolate, adoption, paleontology, computer graphics cards, and various musical artists.

Joining a mailing list is called *subscribing*, and people who subscribe are called *members* or *subscribers* of the mailing list. While you are a member, you'll receive every email message sent to the mailing list, and you can send messages too. If you decide later that you don't want to be a member, you *unsubscribe*.

Mailing lists are somewhat private, since only the members receive messages. (In principle, anybody can join most lists, though.) If you want to open up a discussion to the rest of the online world, this is not practical with a mailing list. Newsgroups, which we'll discuss soon, are much better for this purpose. Some people prefer the relative privacy of mailing lists, however, because they are usually more closely focused on their topics.

What do you like about mailing lists?

- I like that I'm communicating with usually a small group of people (tens or hundreds) with a common interest. Mailing lists tend to be much more topically focused with a lot less "noise" than Usenet newsgroups. —Harv Laser

- They're a great way to meet like-minded people and to gather information from experts on a topic. They can also be helpful for moral or emotional support. —Kathleen Callaway

- I like having targeted information delivered directly to my mailbox. —Ellie Cutler

- One-on-one communication with list members. More than half the responses I make to mailing list posts are personal, directly to the sender. —Bob Parker

SUBSCRIBE TO A MAILING LIST OF INTEREST

To join a mailing list, send an email message containing a request to subscribe. Every mailing list has at least two addresses associated with it:

- *The subscription address*, where you send requests to subscribe and unsubscribe.
- *The list address*, where you send messages that you want all members to read.

Don't mix up these two addresses! When you want to subscribe or unsubscribe, *make sure* to use the subscription address, not the list address. Otherwise, your subscription request will be sent to every member of the list—perhaps thousands of people—who will grumble about "clueless new users." Everybody makes this mistake some time (I remember when I did . . . whew), but try to avoid it.

Subscriptions are sometimes handled by a human being, called the *list maintainer*, and sometimes by a computer program. If subscriptions are handled by a human, ask to subscribe to the list. Make sure to include your email address, in case your return address doesn't get received properly by the list maintainer:

```
To: pig-latin-request@oink.net
Subject: Please subscribe me

Please subscribe me to the Pig Latin mailing list.
My email address is plinky@smoke.com. Anksthay!
```

If subscriptions are handled by a computer program, you'll have to write your subscription request in a particular way that the program can understand. Unfortunately, there is no single "standard" way to write a subscription request, but they usually have one of the following forms:

- The word SUBSCRIBE, followed by your email address.
- The word SUBSCRIBE, followed by your real name.
- The word SUBSCRIBE, followed by the name of the mailing list.
- The word SUBSCRIBE, followed by the name of the mailing list, followed by your email address or real name.

When you discover a mailing list, you'll generally also find subscription instructions that tell you which (if any) of the above forms to use. Here's an example that uses the last form above:

```
To: pig-latin-request@oink.net
Subject: [intentionally left blank]

SUBSCRIBE pig-latin plinky@smoke.com
```

In response to your subscription request, you'll usually receive an email message explaining the purpose of the mailing list, how to send messages to the members, and how to unsubscribe. Save this message! It might be your only instructions for how to unsubscribe.

Speaking of unsubscribing, this is done by sending another email message to the subscription address. It generally has the same form as the subscription message, except that the word SUBSCRIBE is replaced by UNSUBSCRIBE. Again, the technique varies from list to list.

Unsubscribing might not work if you subscribe from one email address, change addresses, and attempt to unsubscribe from your new address. If you encounter this difficulty, write to the list maintainer for assistance.

Some mailing lists allow people to subscribe via the Web, using a fill-in-the-blanks form on a Web page. Expect this subscription style to become more common.

Mailing list dos and don'ts

- DO trim quotes—quote only what is absolutely necessary.

- DON'T quote back a whole message and add "me too" at the end.

- DON'T send requests for subscribing and unsubscribing to the whole list membership. Use the subscription address.

- DO choose wisely between replying to the sender of a message or to the whole mailing list.

- DO change or cancel your mailing list subscriptions when your email address changes or expires.

VISIT A LIST OF MAILING LISTS

So now you know how to join mailing lists. How do you find one devoted to your topic of choice? One way is to post a note in a related newsgroup, asking, "Hey, is there a mailing list devoted to...?" But a faster way is to browse a *list of mailing lists*.

It's hard to keep track of all the mailing lists on the Internet, but some people make a valiant effort. One of the more popular lists of mailing lists is *Publicly Accessible Mailing Lists* (PAML), maintained by Stephanie da Silva. On PAML, you can locate mailing lists by name and by subject. It's available on the Web at:

http://www.neosoft.com/internet/paml/

or by FTP from *rtfm.mit.edu* in the directory:

/pub/usenet/news.answers/mail/mailing-lists/

and it's posted regularly in *news.lists* on Usenet.

Since there is no central authority that tracks mailing lists on the Internet, no "list of lists" will be 100 percent accurate. Some subscription information will be out of date, and some lists won't be mentioned at all. If there's no entry for a mailing list devoted to your desired topic, one still might exist. Use ordinary search techniques (Chapter 5) to check around some more. Or you can even start your own mailing list; see Chapter 11.

Case Study: Find a mailing list on ballroom dancing

- At AltaVista, I gave the query `"ballroom dancing" + "mailing list"`. The first hit looked like it might be relevant but unfortunately was in Japanese! The second hit led to a list of mailing lists, which yielded the desired information. —Ellie Cutler

- I looked in the Usenet newsgroup *rec.arts.dance* but didn't find anything, so I went to Lycos and searched for `ballroom`. One of the hits pointed me to a mailing list at MIT. —Robert Strandh

- I searched AltaVista for `"ballroom dancing" + "mailing list"` and got a few hits. One of them was a guy's home page with dancing tips, and he referred to a mailing list. I'd probably email the guy to ask how to subscribe. —Harv Laser

SOME MAILING LISTS ARE AVAILABLE IN DIGEST FORM

If you join a mailing list that's very active or has many subscribers, you may find your mailbox deluged with email from the list. Some mailing lists resolve this problem by sending messages to subscribers only once a day, once a week, or at other regular intervals, packaged as a *digest*. A digest contains multiple messages, packed together into a single email message. If this interests you, check whether your mailing list has a digest version available. If it does, the information is probably found in the introductory notice you received when you subscribed. Otherwise, ask the list maintainer.

NEWSGROUPS ARE PUBLIC DISCUSSION GROUPS

A Brief Guide to Social Newsgroups and Mailing Lists

news.announce.newusers.

You can find general information about socializing on Usenet and by email in this article written by Dave Taylor. It's posted regularly in the Usenet newsgroup above.

Another great place to meet kindred spirits is Usenet, which we discussed in Chapter 2. Like mailing lists, Usenet newsgroups serve as gathering places for people with mutual interests. Unlike mailing lists, Usenet discussions are open to everybody, not just "members." As a result, the readership of a newsgroup is generally much larger than that of a mailing list, and it's common for discussions to get far off topic. Regardless, a newsgroup can be a great place to find people who share your interests.

How can you find out if there's a Usenet newsgroup devoted to your favorite topic? Use your newsreader to search for newsgroup names that contain a given word. For example, if you want to find a newsgroup devoted to opera, search for `opera`. Each newsreader has a different way to perform this search. The section "Newsreaders can locate newsgroup names" in Chapter 4 has more details.

Another way to search is to connect to the *Usenet Info Center*, at the URL:

http://sunsite.unc.edu/usenet-i/

The Usenet Info Center contains descriptions of many newsgroups and lets you search for newsgroups devoted to particular topics. Keep in mind, however, that not every Internet site receives every newsgroup. The system administrators of your online service provider decide which newsgroups are received. If you want to read a newsgroup that isn't available at your site, talk to your system administrator.

ONLINE SERVICE PROVIDERS MIGHT HAVE LOCAL NEWSGROUPS

Your online service provider might have newsgroups set up for its paid subscribers' use. These newsgroups may be given a different label, such as "message boards," "forums," or "discussion groups." Here is how to locate these resources on the major online service providers:

- *America Online*: Most areas contain "message boards" devoted to their topic.
- *CompuServe*: Most areas contain "forums" devoted to their topic.
- *Microsoft Network*: From the Communicate menu, choose MSN Forums. Also, some areas contain "forums" or "bulletin boards" devoted to their topic.
- *Prodigy*: Use the jumpword `interest groups`.
- *Usenet*: Ask your system staff if any local newsgroups are available at your site.

CHAT GROUPS ALLOW REAL- TIME "TALKING"

A *chat group* is an online meeting place where you can converse with a group of other people. Unlike mailing lists and newsgroups, chat groups are "live", that is, all the participants may talk at the same time. This talking, naturally enough, is called *live chat*. If you are already familiar with chat groups, feel free to skip to the end of the chapter (read the last section and try the quiz).

Chat groups are primarily recreational, designed for meeting other users and holding conversations. They tend to be less informative than newsgroups or mailing lists. But sometimes a quick way to get a question answered, or to get a pointer to information, is to ask in a relevant chat group.

To picture how live chat works, imagine that you are in a crowded room, surrounded by people, all talking. Now imagine that they are typing on keyboards instead, with the words appearing on a large screen for everybody to see. In other words, when you "speak" (by typing something on your keyboard), your words become visible to everybody else in the chat group. In order to keep the conversation understandable, the chat software automatically displays the name of

Netiquette Guidelines
http://www.cis.ohio-state. edu/htbin/rfc/rfc1855.html

A guide to Net etiquette, or responsible behavior on the Net, is available at this site.

the speaker. As an example, let's listen in on a "discussion" about personal computers:

```
<sam> My hard drive just died. Anybody know a good
repair service in the Boston area?
<cathy> BLAZEMONGER is the best computer game I've ever
played! Anybody want some hints?
*** miroslav has just joined
<miroslav> Hi gang!
<spike> cathy: Definitely! How do you get past the
Emerald Guardian??
<peachtree> sam: Try Marv's Micros on Boylston St.
<cathy> Hi miroslav!
<miroslav> What's the best 17" monitor to get?
<sam> peachtree: Much appreciated. Are they expensive?
```

Let's take a closer look at this "discussion." There are five participants: *sam*, *cathy*, *spike*, *peachtree*, and one late arrival, *miroslav*. The name at the beginning of each line, inside angled brackets, identifies the speaker and is displayed automatically by the chat software. These names are often nicknames chosen by the participants.

CHAT DISCUSSIONS CAN OCCUR OUT OF SEQUENCE

You probably noticed that the sentences in the above "discussion" are mixed up or in the wrong order. This is because several conversations are going on at the same time, and several people are typing at once. On your screen, these conversations become *interleaved*, that is, every conversation has bits of other conversations stuck in the middle. Another reason for the strange ordering is that everybody's words are coming to you from different computers scattered around the Internet—some near, some far—so they can arrive at unpredictable times.

In this "discussion," there are actually three separate conversations going on. *sam* and *peachtree* are talking about hard drive repair. If you look only at *sam*'s and *peachtree*'s words, the conversation will become clear:

```
<sam> My hard drive just died. Anybody know a good
repair service in the Boston area?
<peachtree> sam: Try Marv's Micros on Boylston St.
<sam> peachtree: Much appreciated. Are they expensive?
```

(Notice that *sam* and *peachtree* type each other's nickname to help make the flow of the conversation more understandable.) Similarly, *cathy* and *spike* are talking about computer games, and *miroslav* is trying to start a conversation about monitors. This might all look confusing at first, but believe me, you get used to it quickly.

CHAT GROUPS ARE AVAILABLE FROM VARIOUS SERVICES

Your online service provider may have chat groups available to its subscribers. They might be called chats, chat rooms, forums, live

---

Local chat groups

- *America Online*: Use the keyword `people`.

- *CompuServe*: `GO CHAT`.

- *Microsoft Network*: From the Communiacte menu, choose Chat World..

- *Prodigy*: Jumpword `chat` visits the regular chat groups. Jumpword `pseudo` visits the adult-oriented chat groups.

IRC

IRC channels can be created at any time by any IRC user, so there cannot be a definitive list of IRC channels. While running the irc program, you can display a list of active channels with the command:

`/list`

If you want channels that have at least 20 people using them, type:

`/list -min 20`

(or, similarly, any other number than 20).

Another place to find information about individual channels is, strangely enough, the Web. Some channels have been around long enough that the regular members have put together a Web page devoted to the channel. Check out:

http://www.yahoo.com/Computers_and_Internet/Internet/Chatting/IRC/ Channels/

where you'll find links to Web pages devoted to hundreds of individual chat groups.

Finding chat groups of interest

talk, people-to-people chat, or other names. Only subscribers are permitted to participate in these chat groups, and some groups may be restricted to users 18 years and older. See the sidebar "Finding chat groups of interest" for information on how to locate chat groups.

Internet Relay Chat FAQ
http://www.kei.com/irc.html

More information on IRC can be found in this FAQ.

To communicate with a wider audience, consider using a chat service open to the entire Internet. *Internet Relay Chat* (IRC) is one such service accessible from many online service providers. Its chat groups are called *channels*, and each channel is devoted to a particular topic. For example, science fiction television shows are discussed in *#star_trek*, Apple computers are discussed in *#macintosh*, and you can guess what is discussed in *#hotsex*. (Actually, you're probably wrong. The channel names are often completely unrelated to the topics that get discussed. We're only human, after all....) You can also create your own channels and invite other users to join you.

CHOOSE THE MEDIUM THAT SUITS YOUR NEEDS

Mailing lists, newsgroups, and chat groups each have advantages and disadvantages. Mailing lists are great for getting to know a group of people who are avidly devoted to a given topic. On the down side, discussions are conducted by email, and when lots of people participate, your electronic mailbox can fill up rapidly. Usenet newsgroups have a larger set of participants, and this fact brings with it the good and bad points of large groups: more diversity, but less focus. Also, since newsgroups are separate from email, you won't be interrupted every time a new message arrives. Chat groups offer the least amount of raw information, but some people prefer live chatting to the non-real-time conversations on email and Usenet. Table 8-1 summarizes the advantages and disadvantages of these three discussion media.

Fortunately, you can use a combination of these resources to meet people and discuss topics of interest.

Medium	Advantages	Disadvantages
Mailing lists	Semi-private discussion, more focus on topic.	Can overload your mailbox with email if there's no digest version.
Newsgroups	Open discussion, more participants, non-email.	Open discussion, more participants.
Chat groups	Real-time discussion.	Chaotic, less informative.

TABLE 8-1
Discussion media

QUIZ: Finding kindred spirits

1. PAML is not the only list of mailing lists. Can you find others?

2. Can you locate a mailing list devoted to your occupation or hobby? If so, what is the subscription address? What is the list address? Use PAML (or any other list of mailing lists) to answer this question.

3. Repeat question 2, but this time don't use a list of mailing lists. Instead, do a Web search on the name of the occupation or hobby, and follow links to locate mailing list information.

4. Pick any topic of interest, and find out if there is a mailing list devoted to it. Use any method you like.

5. Try to locate a Usenet newsgroup devoted to the same topic as in question 4.

6. Does your online service provider have private mailing lists for its paid subscribers only? Can you find a list of them? How do you join one?

7. What local chat groups, if any, are available from your online service provider? Can you locate a list of them? Can you locate one devoted to a topic you enjoy?

8. Can you connect to IRC from your online service provider?

Finding Freely Distributable Software

9

In this chapter, we'll cover general methods for locating freely distributable software for any computer:

- Searching by platform.

- Searching by category.

- Searching by program name.

- Searching by author.

- Searching by computer.

- Searching by filename.

FREELY DISTRIBUTABLE SOFTWARE IS ON THE INTERNET

No matter what kind of computer you use, there is a wealth of *freely distributable* software available for it on the Internet. "Freely distributable" means that anybody may make copies of the software and give them away, so this software is often placed on Web and FTP sites for anybody to download. The most common kinds of freely distributable software are freeware, shareware, and public domain software (see sidebar), and they are all available in abundance on the Net.

Freely distributable software can be found by various methods:

- *Searching by platform.* If you know what kind of computer and operating system you're using (MS-DOS, Windows, Macintosh, Amiga, Atari, UNIX, etc.), you can locate and browse collections of software for that computer platform.

- *Searching by category.* If you know what kind of program you need (e.g., a word processor, a virus checker), you can use traditional search techniques to locate software of that type.

- *Searching by program name.* If you know the name of the program you need, you can use traditional search techniques to locate a copy.

- *Searching by author.* If you know who wrote a program, you can use traditional name-searching techniques (Chapter 7) to locate the people behind the software.

- *Searching by computer.* If you know the name of the computer where the software is stored, you can jump right to it with FTP.

- *Searching by filename.* Even if you know the name of a program, the program might be stored as an "archive file," under a different name. We'll discuss how to deal with this discrepancy and how to search for files with Archie.

I must stress that commercial programs are *not* freely distributable, even if they are made available "free" by dishonest people (software pirates) on the Net. Software piracy is illegal.

Finally, always use a virus checking program to examine all software that you download or obtain from friends. Be sure to keep your virus checking program up to date by obtaining the latest version on a regular basis.

- *Public domain*: Freely distributable without any copyright restrictions. The author has no control over distribution.

- *Freeware*: Freely distributable, but copyrights are still owned by the author. The author may control distribution.

- *Shareware*: Freely distributable, but if you decide to keep it, you're obligated to pay a fee.

- *GNU General Public License (GPL)*: Freely distributable, and you cannot restrict anybody else from distributing the software freely. (A copy of the license is distributed with all GPL software.)

- *Demoware:* A limited "demo" version of a commercial program, made available by the company, to try before you buy. Often has an expiration date after which the program ceases to function.

Freely distributable software

SOME ONLINE SERVICE PROVIDERS HAVE FILE LIBRARIES

Before searching the Internet for a program, check any file libraries maintained by your online service provider. Downloading may be quicker, and the files may have already been checked for viruses.

- *America Online*: For PC software, use keyword `pcsoftware`. For Macintosh software, use keyword `macsoftware`.

- *CompuServe*: `GO FILEFINDER`.

- *Microsoft Network*: From the Find menu choose Browse All of MSN. Select Subject, then Computers, and then Shareware..

- *Prodigy*: Use the jumpword `file libraries`. If you prefer a Web user interface, use the jumpword `file cabinet`.

SOME WEB SITES SPECIALIZE IN FINDING SOFTWARE

A convenient way to locate software online is to use a Web search engine specially tailored for software. To locate a program, enter some keywords, such as the type of computer, type of program, and name of program, and the search engine retrieves a list of programs that match your needs. Select a program on the list, and it's downloaded onto your computer.

At press time, popular sites of this type are:

http://www.shareware.com

http://www.jumbo.com

Sites like these tend to be helpful and user-friendly, but they catalog only a portion of the software available on the Internet. In the years to come, however, expect sites like these to grow and become the major means for locating freely distributable software on the Net, eventually making the rest of this chapter obsolete.

SOME WEB SITES ARE INDEXES OF SOFTWARE COLLECTIONS

While the previous sites supply a search engine for locating software by keyword, others act as indexes, providing links to dozens or hundreds of software collections. Such indexes usually organize their links by platform: Windows software, Macintosh software, UNIX software, and so on.

At press time, some popular sites of this type are:

http://www.simtel.net/archive/

http://www.jumbo.com

http://filepile.com

These index sites are comprehensive, but they put the burden of searching on you. To locate a particular Windows program, for example, you'd visit the first Windows site in the index and search it, then search the second Windows site, then the third, and so on. There's no master search utility provided for checking all the sites. Even so, these indexes can be very useful for introducing you to previously unknown software collections on the Net.

SEARCH BY PLATFORM TO LOCATE SOFTWARE COLLECTIONS

To locate software for your favorite computer platform, there are several ways to proceed. You could do a Web search for the platform name (`windows`, `macintosh`, etc.), but you're likely to get many irrelevant hits. Freely distributable software is just one of many computer-related topics. Instead, try a more specific search, like:

```
Windows AND (freeware OR shareware OR "public domain")
```

This kind of query can help you locate collections of software for your preferred computer.

A quicker, more reliable method than Web searching may be to investigate the Usenet newsgroups devoted to your platform of choice. Table 9-1 shows sample platforms and their corresponding newsgroups. (The blanks indicate that multiple newsgroups are devoted to this computer platform.)

Platform	Usenet Newsgroups
Acorn	*comp.sys.acorn._____*
Amiga	*comp.sys.amiga. _____*
Apple II	*comp.sys.apple2. _____*
Atari	*comp.sys.atari. _____*
Commodore 64/128	*comp.sys.cbm*
Linux	*comp.os.linux. _____*
Macintosh	*comp.sys.mac. _____*
Newton	*comp.sys.newton. _____*
NeXT	*comp.sys.next. _____*
OS/2	*comp.os.os2. _____*
Windows	*comp.os.ms-windows. _____*
Windows NT	*comp.os.ms-windows.nt. _____*
UNIX	*comp.unix. _____*

TABLE 9-1
Platform newsgroups

In particular, the newsgroups may have an FAQ (Frequently Asked Questions document) that lists the best Internet sites for freely distributable software. FAQs are posted in the newsgroups regularly, and many are also available by anonymous FTP from *rtfm.mit.edu*. In the directory /pub/usenet, you'll find the FAQs arranged by newsgroup name. On the Web, this directory is found at:

ftp://rtfm.mit.edu/pub/usenet/

If you append a newsgroup name and a slash onto this URL, like so:

ftp://rtfm.mit.edu/pub/usenet/comp.sys.mac.misc/

you'll jump directly to the FAQs for that newsgroup, if they exist. You can also browse FAQs at the URL:

ftp://rtfm.mit.edu/pub/usenet-by-hierarchy/

See Chapter 4 for other ways of finding FAQs.

Finally, don't forget about computer user groups in your community. They can be a great source of freely distributable software and other helpful information about your computer. Your local computer retailer may know of some user groups.

SEARCH BY CATEGORY WHEN YOU DON'T KNOW A SPECIFIC PROGRAM

Another way to search for software is by category: word processor, virus utility, paint program, 3D graphics program, and so on. This is a good idea when you know what kind of program you want, but you don't know which ones are available. Once again, traditional Web search techniques can come in handy for queries like `"word processor"` and `"virus checker"`.

You might receive many irrelevant hits because the queries are too general. Then again, you might locate a software collection devoted to your category. One never knows.

Searching by category and platform simultaneously can increase your chances of locating the software you want:

```
"word processor" AND (MS-DOS OR MSDOS)
```

Yahoo provides a convenient list of links for locating software by category:

http://www.yahoo.com/Computers_and_Internet/Software/

SEARCH BY NAME TO LOCATE A PARTICULAR PROGRAM

If you know the name of a program, then traditional Web search techniques, with queries and keywords, may be your best bet for locating it quickly. For example, to locate the program SuperStuff, make a query with the keyword `SuperStuff`.

This method might not work well if the program name is a common word, like Edit, that's likely to appear in many unrelated Web pages. In this case, you can try making the query more specific by adding keywords related to computer programs: `shareware`, `version`, the computer platform, and so on, to try to reduce the number of irrelevant hits:

`Edit AND shareware AND Macintosh AND version`

SEARCH BY AUTHOR'S NAME

If you know the name of a program's author, use the search techniques in Chapter 7 to locate the program. This technique is particularly useful if you own a program by that author and want to find out if he or she has written any other programs. (Also check the program documentation for the author's email address and/or home page.)

USE FTP IF YOU KNOW A PROGRAM'S LOCATION

FTP, introduced in Chapter 2, copies files between computers. To use FTP, you generally need to know the name of the computer where the files reside. The next section explains how to connect to a computer and transfer files.

Most FTP sites have a file that describes the site briefly. It typically has the word "README" in its name: README, READ.ME,

FTP FAQ
http://ftp.wustl.edu/
~aminet/ftpfaq

Further details on FTP are available at this site

00-README, README.1ST, etc. Download and read this file before using the FTP site any further.

Many FTP sites also have an index file that lists the available files at the site. Downloading and reading this file can save time, compared to randomly browsing around the FTP site. The "README" file should indicate the location of the index file.

Traditionally, public files on FTP sites are kept in a directory (folder) called *pub*. If you connect to an FTP site and don't see any files available, look first in the *pub* directory.

FTP MAY BE ANONYMOUS

Anonymous FTP lets anybody download software from an Internet computer, provided the computer permits anonymous FTP connections. To use anonymous FTP, you'll need to know:

- The name of the computer you want to contact: the FTP site.
- The anonymous FTP username, *anonymous*.
- The anonymous FTP password. By tradition, use your email address as the password. (Not your login password! Your email address: *you@your.machine*.) This politely lets the FTP site maintainer know who is using his/her resources.
- The location, on the FTP site computer, of the files you want to download.

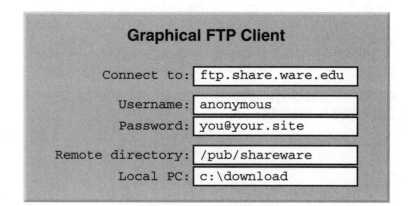

FIGURE 9-1:
A graphical FTP program's login window

Modern FTP programs have graphical user interfaces that prompt you for the first three items, wait for you to click "OK," and log you in, as in Figure 9-1.

Once you are connected, a graphical FTP program presents you with a list of available files and directories (folders). Using a point-and-click interface, you navigate the FTP site, looking for the files you want. When you find them, typically you double-click on their names or press a "download" button.

You can also download files by anonymous FTP using your Web browser. If the name of the anonymous FTP site is *cool.site.edu*, put *ftp://* in front of it, and tell your browser to connect to:

ftp://cool.site.edu

Now you can download files using a familiar Web interface—no login required.

OLDER FTP PROGRAMS USE COMMAND LINES

Command-line interfaces are still found on some FTP programs. Their use is a bit cryptic but sometimes more powerful than using a graphical program or Web browser. They can upload files (unlike some Web browsers), and they can download multiple files with a single command (unlike Web browsers and some graphical programs), as we will discuss soon.

Run the program, giving the name of the FTP site as an argument:

```
ftp cool.site.edu
```

You're then prompted for the anonymous FTP username and password:

```
Connected to cool.site.edu
220 cool.site.edu FTP server (UNIX(r) System V Release
4.0) ready.
Name (cool.site.edu:username):
```

Type the anonymous FTP username, anonymous, and press RETURN. FTP then prompts you for the password:

```
331 Password required for anonymous:
```

Type your email address. If all is well, then you'll be logged in:

```
230 User anonymous logged in.
*** Welcome to the Cool FTP Site! Download the file ***
README for help.
ftp>
```

The prompt *ftp>* indicates that FTP is ready to accept commands. The important commands for downloading files are shown in Table 9-2.

Notice the mget command downloads many files with a single command. This is typically not possible with a Web browser—you must download each file individually by selecting its link. Some graphical FTP programs permit multi-file downloads; check the documentation. Multi-file downloads are great when you have a lot to download and don't want to sit in front of the computer all day, clicking buttons for each file.

ARCHIE SEARCHES FOR FTP FILES BY FILENAME

With so many anonymous FTP sites on the Internet, locating a particular file can be a chore. Enter *Archie*, a gigantic database of Internet files that are available for downloading. Ask Archie about a file, and Archie tells you where it can be found, assuming that Archie has heard of it.

Archie works only for file *names*, however. It's not a general search utility like a Web search engine. If you're looking for a program called SuperStuff, but it's stored as an archive file called ss.zip, a search for SuperStuff could be fruitless. Archie will know only the name ss.zip. (See the next section for more information on archives.)

To locate an Archie Web page, do a Web search for archie or look on the List of WWW Archie Services at:

http://pubweb.nexor.co.uk/public/archie/servers.html

Some current Archie Web pages are:

http://www-ns.rutgers.edu/htbin/archie

http://hoohoo.ncsa.uiuc.edu/archie.html

http://www.ucc.ie/cgi-bin/archie

Command	Example	Meaning
get	get myfile.txt	Download one file, in this case, `myfile.txt`.
mget	mget *.zip	Download multiple files, in this case, every file with a name ending in `.zip`. An asterisk matches anything. A question mark matches any one character.
binary	binary	Turn on binary mode. Type this command once before downloading non-text files such as archive files (discussed later) and programs.
put	put myfile.txt	Upload one file, in this case, `myfile.txt`.
mput	mput *.zip	Upload multiple files, analogous to mget.
prompt	prompt	Normally, mget and mput prompt you before each file is transferred, and you type `yes` or `no` in response. The prompt command turnsthis prompting off. To turn it back on, type `prompt` again.
cd	cd software	Change directory, in this case, go to the directory called `software`.
cd	cd ..	Move one directory up or backward.
help	help	See a list of FTP commands.
help	help get	See a short explanation of a particular command, in this case, get.
quit	quit	End the FTP session.

TABLE 9-2:
Commands for downloading files

The user interface on these pages is similar to that of Web search engines. Some not only locate files but also provide Web links to them for convenient downloading.

Archie is powerful but slow. Unlike modern Web searches, Archie searches may take several minutes to complete.

Archie doesn't know about all files on the Internet. It's a "passive" service, roughly like the passive search engines we saw in Chapter 5. Files have to be registered with Archie, or else they'll be unknown—absent from Archie's database. Fortunately, FTP site maintainers around the world regularly register files with Archie.

Note that Archie isn't limited to locating software. It can locate any FTP site files: academic papers, documentation, and so on.

PROGRAMS MAY BE PACKAGED AS ARCHIVES

Information on archive formats can be found at:

http://alpha.rollanet.org/library/FileFormats.html

http://www.cs.brown.edu/stc/summer/workshop/summer_archives.html

http://www.matisse.net/files/formats.html

Some software consists of multiple files: the program itself, documentation, examples, shareware registration forms, and other support files. To keep these files together for convenient uploading and downloading, software developers use programs called *archivers*. An archiver "packs" multiple files into a single file, called an *archive*. When you download an archive, you "unpack" the files using a *de-archiver* program.

Archives are usually recognized by their names. For example, a zip archive name ends with the characters `.zip`. Table 9-3 shows how to recognize some popular archive formats.

De-archiving programs can be obtained from freely distributable software sites, CD-ROMs of freely distributable software, friends, and user groups. The list below shows some well-known archivers and the official locations for their de-archiving programs.

gzip	*ftp://prep.ai.mit.edu/pub/gnu/*
lha	*ftp://ftp.wustl.edu/pub/aminet/util/arc/*
PKZIP	*http://www.pkware.com*
Stuffit Expander	*http://www.aladdinsys.com*
tar	(a standard UNIX program)
uncompress	(a standard UNIX program)
WinZip	*http://www.winzip.com*

Name ends with...	Archive format	Most popular on...
.zip	Zip	PC. De-archive with PKZIP, WinZip, ...
.exe	Self-extracting	PC. No de-archiving program needed. Just run the file like a program.
.hqx	BinHex	Macintosh. De-archive with Stuffit Expander.
.sea	Stuffit	Macintosh. De-archive with Stuffit Expander.
.Z	Compress	UNIX. De-archive with uncompress.
.gz	GNU gzip	UNIX. De-archive with gzip.
.tar	tar	UNIX. De-archive with tar.
.lha	LhA	Amiga. De-archive with lha.

TABLE 9-3:
Popular archive formats

QUIZ: Finding freely distributable software

1. Locate a newsgroup devoted to your preferred computer platform. Subscribe to it and read some articles. Does the newsgroup have an FAQ? Check *rtfm.mit.edu* to find out.

2. Locate a virus checking program for your preferred computer platform. If you don't already have one installed, download and install it.

3. Locate a shareware word processor that runs under Windows 95.

4. Locate a freeware screensaver program that runs on the Macintosh.

5. Locate a freely distributable program that sets your computer's clock to the same time as a super-accurate atomic clock on the Internet.

6. Do you use any of the archiver programs listed in this chapter? If so, use traditional Web search techniques to find the version number of the latest version. (And download the latest version if you don't have it.)

7. Select your favorite freely distributable program. Try to locate the home page of the author.

8. Do you own any freely distributable programs that you aren't completely satisfied with? If so, try to locate and download another program of the same type. Try it out; maybe you'll like it better than the one you're using.

Finding Information Again

10

As you explore the Internet, you're sure to find favorite places that you'll visit regularly. If you discover these sites after long searching, however, you certainly won't want to redo the search every time you want to visit them. This chapter discusses strategies for *revisiting* Internet sites quickly and efficiently.

This chapter covers three major topics:

- *Managing bookmarks*: tips, tricks, pros and cons.

- *When bookmarks go stale:* dealing with change on the Internet. If your favorite Web site moves without warning, you can find it again, sometimes without doing much searching.

- *Moving beyond bookmarks*: making a set of private Web pages to provide quick, organized access to your favorite resources. This is the most technical part of the book.

BOOKMARKS ARE URLS YOUR BROWSER REMEMBERS

General bookmarking tips can be found at:
 http://www.cnet.com/ Resources/Tech/Advisers/ Bookmark/

http://www.signweb.com/ main/netnews/better.html

http://www.technet.nm.org/ ~coach/vpnw/tutorial/ tutl10.htm

All Web browsers have a feature that lets you mark interesting sites so you can return to them easily. This is called *bookmarking* the Web page. To return to the page later, simply select the bookmark. Bookmarks are also called *hotlinks, hotlist items, favorites,* or other names, depending on which browser you use. When you encounter an interesting page, tell the browser to bookmark it. Later, when you want to see the page again, simply select its bookmark, and the browser returns to the page. Bookmarks are terrific time-savers.

It's important to understand how bookmarks work. When you bookmark a Web page, the bookmark does *not* save a copy of the page. It invisibly saves the URL of the page. When you select a bookmark, your browser silently examines the URL and reconnects to the page. In this sense, bookmarks are much like links, except *you* create them.

CHOOSE WHETHER TO BOOKMARK OR COPY

If you find a great Web page and want to refer to it often, which is better: bookmarking the page (i.e., making your browser memorize the URL), or saving a copy of the page on your local disk (using Save or Save As)? It depends. Copying is good for speed reasons; it's faster to access a copy on your hard drive than a page on the other side of the world. Bookmarking is good for having the most up-to-date information; if material on the Web page changes, your bookmark points to the new material, whereas a saved copy will have the old material. Each method has advantages and disadvantages, summarized in Table 10-1.

If you aren't sure whether to bookmark or copy a Web page, here are some questions that may help you decide.

- *Is it important?* Then copy it. If you bookmark a page and it disappears later, you're out of luck.

- *Is it large?* Then it's up to you. If you bookmark it, you'll download the large page many times over repeated visits. If you copy it, you download it only once, but it takes up space on your hard disk.

Characteristic	Bookmarking	Copying	Why?
Access to the page	Less reliable	More reliable	Your local disk is always available, but the network is not.
Speed of access	Slower	Faster	The local disk is faster than thenetwork.
Guaranteed to find it again?	No	Yes	The Net changes.
Latest version of the page?	Yes	Maybe	A saved copy becomes outdated if the original page changes.
Disk space occupied	Less space	More space	Bookmarks are much smaller than files.
Organized how?	Bookmarks	Files	Bookmarks are organized using the browser. Copies are files and are organized using the operating system. You might prefer one method over the other.
Remembers the URL?	Yes	No	When you copy a page to a file, the URL might not be saved in the file. If you later forget where you got the file from, the URL may be hard to rediscover.

TABLE 10-1:
Bookmarking vs. copying

- *Is the information likely to change?* Then bookmark it. For instance, a price list from a store is likely to change often, so a copy would soon be outdated.

- *Do you need to follow other links on it?* Then bookmark it. It doesn't make much sense to copy one page if you'll be regularly accessing its other subpages over the Internet. You could conceivably copy the page and all its subpages, but browsers don't provide much help. You'd have to copy each subpage individually, which is a pain.

One exception to this guideline is that you could copy a page to a disk file, load the file in your browser as a Web page, and voila, you have a local copy of the page with usable links. A friend of mine uses a copy of Yahoo's main page as his startup page so he can access Yahoo's subcategories quickly. Links change, however, so if you do this, check the original page every so often.

- *Does it have graphics that you need to see?* Then bookmark it (or print it). When you copy a page, its graphics are not copied with it. They're still being downloaded over the Internet, and they're probably larger than the page you saved.

- *Is it copyrighted?* Then copying it might not be legal, and book-marking is your only option. Copyright issues on the Web are a sticky subject that's beyond the scope of this book.

More information about Netscape's SmarkMarks is available at:
http://home.netscape.com/comprod/power_pack.html
http://home.netscape.com/home/add_ons/smrtmrks2_0_qstart.html

Finally, if you can't make up your mind, you can choose to bookmark *and* copy the page.

At press time, products for bookmark management are beginning to appear, such as Netscape's SmartMarks, that allow for more convenient bookmarking and copying. A SmartMark keeps a copy of a Web page on your local disk and automatically updates it when the original changes.

BOOKMARKS CAN BE ORGANIZED

Bookmark management for Netscape Navigator is documented in the online *Netscape Navigator Handbook*. To view it, select Handbook from the Help menu.

Every browser has some facility for managing bookmarks that lets you add, move, select, change, rename, and delete bookmarks. Most of them present bookmarks as a list, usually called a bookmark list or hotlist. A well-organized list of carefully named bookmarks is a valuable resource, providing quick access to your favorite pages.

As the number of bookmarks grows, it can become difficult to keep track of them in a single, large list. Some browsers, therefore, are beginning to support multiple bookmark lists, allowing users to organize their bookmarks into categories. For instance, you could have a "Computers" list, a "Music" list, and a "Politics" list with appropriate bookmarks inside each. Taking things a step further, some browsers support *hierarchical* bookmark lists, allowing lists to contain other lists of bookmarks. For instance, your "Music" list could itself contain other lists devoted to classical music and modern music. Both

- My local library, the home page of my laboratory, a daily newspaper in Sweden, a page for conjugating French verbs, and Lycos. —Robert Strandh

- Yahoo, Open Text, and AltaVista. —Kathleen Callaway

- AltaVista, my own Web site, the Postcard Store, Virtual Flowers, and the Clipart Collection. —Fern Dickman

- My home page, the CUCUG Amiga Web Directory, AltaVista, VIScorp, the Internet Movie Database, CNN, and the USGS earthquake maps. —Harv Laser

- AltaVista, the ESPNET Basketball site, and the O'Reilly & Associates home page (which I develop). —Ellie Cutler

What are your most-used bookmarks?

Netscape Navigator and Microsoft Internet Explorer support hierarchical bookmarks.

At press time, many browsers still support only a single list of bookmarks. Later in this chapter, we'll discuss how to get around this limitation.

Bookmark Management for Microsoft Internet Explorer is documented in the programs online manual. Choose Help Topics from the Help menu and look up "bookmarks" or "favorites".

STALE LINKS ARE A FACT OF LIFE

Once you have organized your bookmarks, you can easily jump to all your favorite Web sites…right? Well, usually. Web pages move around, unfortunately, leaving other people's links and bookmarks pointing to outdated locations. Such links are called *stale links*. When you try to follow a stale link, your browser will complain that no page was found at that URL.

You can't avoid stale links, but you can learn how to work around them. The next few sections discuss how to refind a Web page that has moved, and how to choose links that are less likely to go stale. The goal is to save time so when a link goes stale, you don't have to do extensive searching to find the new location.

MAIN PAGES MOVE LESS OFTEN THAN SUBPAGES DO

Most Web sites with more than one page are organized to have a "main" page that leads you to "subpages" with more detailed information. You reach the subpages following the main page's links. (And those subpages may have subpages of their own, and so on.) A main page often has a short URL, ending with a computer name, like this:

http://www.billybobs.com

or ending with a username, like this:

http://www.billybobs.com/~billy/

The URLs of subpages are longer, however, building on the URL of the main page, like these examples:

http://www.billybobs.com/info/fishing/bait/

http://www.billybobs.com/~billy/movies/favorites.html

As a rule, Web site maintainers are reluctant to change the URL of their "main" page; the URL may have name recognition, have appeared in advertisements, and so on. Subpages, however, are fair game for being moved around, renamed, or deleted as maintainers update and improve their Web sites. (Analogy: when you remodel your home, your address doesn't change.)

Thus, if you bookmark a main page, rather than a subpage, your bookmark is less likely to go stale. From the main page, you can then reach the subpage by following links.

This technique is not convenient if you must follow many links to reach a desired subpage. But if the subpage is only one or two links off the main page, then bookmarking the main page might be a good idea.

BOOKMARK A SUBPAGE ALONG WITH ITS MAIN PAGE

Sometimes you *want* to bookmark a subpage because it contains specific information that you need and you aren't interested in the rest of the Web site. For example, suppose you're a chemist and have located a handy periodic table of the elements:

http://www.science-stuff.org/chem/stats/periodic.html

found on a gigantic "science" Web site:

http://www.science-stuff.org

All you need is the table. It would be inconvenient to bookmark the science page and then follow many links to reach the table.

In this case, you can still help to avoid stale links by bookmarking the subpage *and* the main page. When you need the subpage, jump to it by bookmark. If the subpage later goes stale, use the main page's bookmark and try to refind the subpage. In our chemistry example, you could bookmark both the periodic table page and the main science page.

GO TO THE ROOT OF THE URL

Let's say you're an avid fisherman and you have a question about the best kinds of bait to use. After a long and arduous Net search, you locate the information you need at Billy Bob's Bait & Tackle:

http://www.billybobs.com/bait/worms/choosing.html

You spend many happy hours perusing Billy Bob's advice and you return frequently. One day, however, your Web browser tells you "page not found." Your favorite link has gone stale. What should you do?

If a bookmark goes stale, you can sometimes quickly refind the page (assuming it has been moved or renamed, not deleted) by chopping off parts of the URL, from right to left. It's possible that Billy Bob has just reorganized his Web pages, renaming the file `choosing.html` to something else. Strip it from the URL and try:

http://www.billybobs.com/bait/worms/

This URL may lead to information that will help you find the old page. If not, or if no page is found at this URL, repeat the process, stripping off further words from the URL, one at a time, and trying each new URL:

http://www.billybobs.com/bait/

http://www.billybobs.com

The last URL above is likely to be Billy Bob's main Web page. If the main page is gone, then the site has moved or disappeared. This

Uniform Resource Locators (URLs)
http://www.w3.org/pub/ WWW/Addressing/ rfc1738.txt

A very thorough and technical explanation of URLs can be found at this site.

**Case Study:
Intuition saves
the day**

I once used AltaVista to search for a review of a particular book. The search located a page that, according to AltaVista's summary, contained a review of the book. When I connected to the page, however, I found a review of an entirely different book. There wasn't a single mention of my book on the whole page. How strange. Why did AltaVista count this page as a hit, I wondered?

I examined the URL: *http://wwwiz.com/current/wiz_d02.html*. The word "current" made me wonder: perhaps this page is updated frequently with new book reviews. If so, might the old reviews still be around on this Web site?

Acting on a hunch, I connected to the root of the URL, *http://wwwiz.com*, hoping to find a main page for the site. Sure enough, the main page was there, and it had a link labeled Back Issues. Bingo. I selected the link and browsed by eye through summaries of old articles. Soon I found one that looked like the hit AltaVista had located. I selected its link... and there was the desired review.

Why did AltaVista locate the wrong page? Because its catalog was outdated. It still listed the text of the old review, even though the page had been changed to have a new review.

technique doesn't always work, but when it does, it can save time over a full-fledged Net search. By the way, remember to use the computer's cut-and-paste feature to avoid retyping the URLs above.

BOOKMARKS ARE LIMITED

Bookmarks are very handy but not a complete solution. If you have a lot of bookmarks, for instance, they can be awkward to organize. In addition, you might discover interesting resources that are not technically on the Web—FTP sites, Gopher menus, email addresses, and so on—that your browser might not let you bookmark conveniently. Wouldn't it be helpful to have all these sites available from a single place for easy access? Well, you can.

The rest of this chapter discusses a method for organizing all of your favorite Web pages, Usenet newsgroups, email addresses, Gopher

> - Hopefully the page owner will have left behind a link to the new location. If not, I try to find it with a search engine. Lots of pages run by college students go away when they leave school. —Harv Laser
>
> - I look at the bookmarks of my colleagues at work. We've usually been looking for the same sites. —Kathleen Callaway
>
> - I look for it in AltaVista, and if I can't find it, I delete the bookmark. I periodically clean up my bookmarks anyway, just to be tidy. —Fern Dickman
>
> - My bookmarks come and go, just like the newsgroups I read. I often delete an item before it becomes obsolete. —Robert Strandh

How do you refind a vanished resource?

menus, FTP sites, and files in a single place for convenient access, by creating your own set of private Web pages. We'll discuss:

- Special types of URLs for all of the above information sources.

- Organizing these URLs with a Web page construction program.

- Organizing these URLs by hand, by writing HTML code.

This is the most technical material in the book. You needn't read it if:

- You keep only a small number of bookmarks.

- You keep lots of bookmarks, and your browser supports multiple bookmark lists or hierarchical bookmarks to keep them organized.

- Your browser can bookmark FTP sites, Gopher pages, and Usenet newsgroups.

- You don't care about bookmarking email addresses.

- You already know how to make Web pages.

If you fit any of these criteria, feel free to skip ahead to the quiz. On the other hand, if you'd like to organize your bookmarks better, build some simple Web pages, or just learn more about URLs, read on.

Ready? Let's put on our protective headgear and dive right in.

URLS CAN POINT TO MORE THAN WEB PAGES

In Chapter 3, we briefly looked at different forms of URLs. This section explores that material in more detail.

Citing Electronic Resources
*http://libweb.uoregon.edu/
network/citing.html*

*http://www.cas.usf.edu/
english/walker/mla.html*

*http://funnelweb.utcc.utk.edu/
Teltrain/cita.htm*

Sometimes it isn't enough to know where to locate an online resource: you have to tell others where to locate it. A common example is a citation in a research paper. Guidelines for citing online references are still being debated and can be found at these sites.

As we've seen throughout the book, Web page URLs begin with *http://*, followed by a computer name, optionally followed by a path to a Web page file or directory:

http://my.machine.edu/stuff/other/myfile.html

http://my.machine.edu/stuff/other/

Gopher menus can also be accessed by URL. Such URLs are very similar to those of Web pages, but *http* is replaced by *gopher*, like so:

gopher://my.machine.edu/stuff/other/myfile

gopher://my.machine.edu/stuff/other/

Anonymous FTP site URLs begin with *ftp://*, followed by the name of the computer you want to access by FTP, followed by the path to a file or directory:

ftp://my.machine.edu/stuff/other/myfile

ftp://my.machine.edu/stuff/other/

Usenet newsgroups are accessed by simpler URLs. They begin with *news:* (no slashes) and end with the name of a newsgroup:

news:rec.music.classical

news:comp.sys.ibm.pc.hardware

Email addresses can be accessed by URL, beginning with *mailto:* and ending with the email address of the recipient:

mailto:interest-list@my.computer.edu

mailto:dbarrett@ora.com

Finally, you can access local files on your computer's disk by URL. The URL format depends on what kind of computer you're using. See the sidebar, "Files have URLs too", for details.

There are other kinds of URLs, but they aren't important for our purposes in this book.

You can make links to files on your computer, using a URL of the form:

*file://*path

This kind of URL has two parts:

1. *file://*
   All file URLs begin with this.

2. path
   The list of folders or directories that lead to the file on your computer's disk, followed by the filename.

To discover a file's path conveniently on your computer, use your browser's Open File or Open Local command and select the file you want. The URL will then be displayed by the browser.

File paths look slightly different for different operating systems:

- Windows:

  /Drive|/Folder/Folder/Folder/.../File

  For example, if the file `Stuff.txt` is found inside the folder (directory) `MyFolder` immediately inside the disk C:, its URL is:

  file:///C|/MyFolder/Stuff.txt

  A file called `OtherStuff` on the desktop has the URL:

  file:///C|/WINDOWS/DESKTOP/OtherStuff

- Macintosh:

  /Disk/Folder/Folder/Folder/.../File

  For example, if the file `Stuff` is found inside the folder `MyFolder` immediately inside the disk MyDisk, its URL is:

  file:///MyDisk/MyFolder/Stuff

  A file called `OtherStuff` on the desktop has the URL:

  file:///Desktop Folder/OtherStuff

- UNIX:

  localhost/Directory/Directory/.../File

Files have URLs too

YOU CAN ORGANIZE URLS INTO PRIVATE WEB PAGES

Once you know how to write URLs for various kinds of resources, it's time to put them to use. Gather some URLs of your favorite news-groups, FTP sites, Web pages, email addresses, and so on, and organize them into categories: art, science, politics, history, business, animals, food, or whatever you like. Keep the number of categories small for now, no more than five or six.

For each of these categories, you'll be creating a Web page full of links to the related URLs. Once your category Web pages are complete, you'll create a main Web page that points to all of your category pages. Finally, you'll store your main page as a bookmark, so you can view it conveniently. As a final result, you'll have quick, organized access to your favorite resources on a variety of topics.

All of the Web pages you'll make will be private, not available to other people on the Web. They'll be stored on your local computer.

WEB PAGE CONSTRUCTION PROGRAMS CAN HELP

How do you make these private Web pages? If possible, use a Web page construction program. Many such programs exist today, both commercial products and freely distributable software. The list below shows how to create and post Web pages on some major online service providers. Or use the methods of Chapter 9 to locate the latest programs.

- *America Online*: Enter keyword `personal publisher`, where you'll find programs and instructions for creating a Web page. When you create and upload Web pages, Personal Publisher will tell you their URLs.

- *CompuServe*: A program called Home Page Wizard is provided for CompuServe users. Use `GO HPWIZ` to download and use it. Home Page Wizard provides a graphical user interface for building a Web page and uploading it to CompuServe. When you create and upload pages, you'll be told their URLs.

- *Microsoft Network*: Personal Web pages are not supported at press time.

- *Prodigy*: Use jumpword `pwp` (or `personal web pages`) to visit the Personal Web Pages Site Manager. If you already have a way to create Web pages on your home computer, either with HTML (described briefly below) or a Web page construction program, you can upload them to Prodigy here. Select Manage Your Web Site to do this. When finished, you'll be told what your URL is.

  If you don't know how to create Web pages, Prodigy provides a program called Hippie to help you. Download Hippie from the Personal Web Pages Site Manager.

- *UNIX account*: Create a subdirectory called `public_html` in your home directory, using the commands:

```
cd

mkdir public_html

chmod 711 public_html
```

  and copy your Web page files into it. Make sure the files are world-readable (chmod 644).

  If your account is on the computer *www.xyz.org*, your username is *sandy*, and your file in the directory `public_html` is `myfile.html`, then the URL of the page is:

  http://www.xyz.org/~sandy/myfile.html

  Notice that public_html does not appear in the URL.

Web page construction programs use a point-and-click graphical interface to create Web pages. All you need to know are the URLs for the links you want on your pages. The rest is up to your imagination.

CREATE YOUR PRIVATE WEB PAGES

As you create each Web page, store it as a file on your local computer disk. Web page files end with `.html` (on most computers) or `.htm` (on DOS machines). Use filenames that indicate the category of links to be found in the file; for example, `science.html` for science, `movies.html` for movies, and so on.

Once your category Web page files are created, make a main Web page that points to your category pages. This is done in the following way, supposing that your category files are `science.html` and `movies.html`:

1. Make sure all of your category files are in the same folder or directory on your local computer's disk.

2. Create a new Web page file with links to these URLs:

    science.html

    movies.html

    These are the complete URLs, no "http" or anything else. Name the links Science and Movies, or anything else you like.

3. Store your main Web page file in the same directory as the category files. Call it whatever you like, for example, `main.html`.

4. Quit the Web page construction program.

5. Using your browser, use the Open File or Open Local command to view your file `main.html`.

6. Tell your browser to make a bookmark.

Voila! You now have a private Web page, easily accessible from a bookmark, that leads to your organized category pages. Figure 10-1 illustrates what your pages might look like.

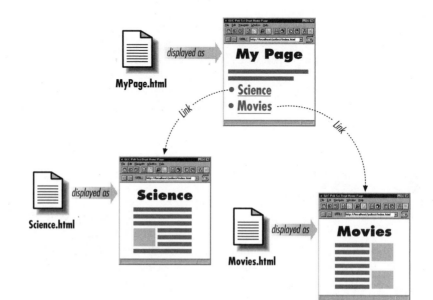

FIGURE **10-1:**
Your private Web pages

HTML IS THE LANGUAGE OF WEB PAGES

If you don't have access to a Web page construction program, you can still make Web pages, but the process is a bit more technical. To make a Web page, you create an ordinary text file with special commands in it, written in a language called HTML (HyperText Markup Language). This section will show you just enough HTML to make some basic Web pages.

Disclaimer: For simplicity, I have omitted some important aspects of HTML in the following discussion. You'll learn to produce minimal Web pages that are good enough for organizing bookmarks, but not complete enough to be considered "good HTML." If you plan on making Web pages for the public, or if you want more information on HTML, I recommend reading a real HTML book or doing a Yahoo search for `HTML tutorial`.

HTML CONSISTS OF TEXT AND TAGS

HTML has two parts:

- Ordinary text.

- Special text, called *tags*, that describe how your ordinary text should appear on the Web page. Tags are instructions to the Web browser, explaining how the page should look.

Tags look like words enclosed in angled brackets, like this:

```
<TITLE>
<MENU>
<P>
```

The angled brackets tell the Web browser that it should display the Web page in a certain way. You can read them as, "Hey, browser, here's an instruction for you!"

Most tags have two parts: a beginning and an end. For example, if you wanted your Web page to have the title "My Favorite Links," you would write the HTML commands:

```
<TITLE>
My Favorite Links
</TITLE>
```

The first tag, <TITLE>, means, "Hey, browser, the following text is a title, so display it like one." The second tag, </TITLE>, means, "Hey, browser, the title is finished." When a Web browser displays a file with this HTML in it, the title ("My Favorite Links") is displayed properly by the browser, and the HTML commands do not appear on the screen.

In general, a tag that has a slash before the word means "finished," as in </TITLE> ("Hey, browser, the title is finished"). Some tags, however, have only one part instead of two. For instance, if you want to make a paragraph of text, the HTML is:

```
<P>
This is a paragraph of text. It's
a very nice paragraph and I expect it will win
major
awards.
```

In this case, <P> means "Hey, browser, display the following text as a nicely justified paragraph." No </P> tag is needed to end the paragraph.

Table 10-2 shows some common tags to use when creating your private Web pages.

Figure 10-2 shows a short HTML file, both as plain text and as it would be displayed by a Web browser. We have just scratched the surface of HTML in this section, but it should be enough to get you started.

Item	Begin With	Continue With	End With
Page title	<TITLE>	Your title text	</TITLE>
Heading	<H1>	Your heading text	</H1>
Link	<A HREF= "URL goes here">	Your link text	</A>
List of choices	<MENU>	Your choices	</MENU>
One menu choice	<LI>	Any text	
Paragraph of text	<P>	Any text	

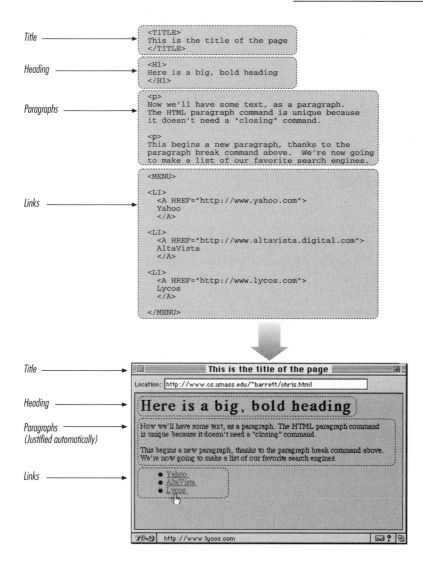

Title

```
<TITLE>
This is the title of the page
</TITLE>
```

Heading

```
<H1>
Here is a big, bold heading
</H1>
```

Paragraphs

```
<p>
Now we'll have some text, as a paragraph.
The HTML paragraph command is unique because
it doesn't need a "closing" command.

<p>
This begins a new paragraph, thanks to the
paragraph break command above.  We're now going
to make a list of our favorite search engines.
```

Links

```
<MENU>

<LI>
  <A HREF="http://www.yahoo.com">
  Yahoo
  </A>

<LI>
  <A HREF="http://www.altavista.digital.com">
  AltaVista
  </A>

<LI>
  <A HREF="http://www.lycos.com">
  Lycos
  </A>

</MENU>
```

Title

Heading

Paragraphs
(Justified automatically)

Links

This is the title of the page

Location: http://www.cs.umass.edu/~barrett/chris.html

Here is a big, bold heading

Now we'll have some text, as a paragraph. The HTML paragraph command is unique because it doesn't need a "closing" command.

This begins a new paragraph, thanks to the paragraph break command above. We're now going to make a list of our favorite search engines.

- Yahoo
- AltaVista
- Lycos

http://www.lycos.com

FIGURE 10-2
An HTML example

LINKS ARE YOUR MOST IMPORTANT HTML TAGS

To create a link using HTML, you must know the URL where you want the link to point. For instance, to make a link that points to the O'Reilly & Associates Web site, you need to know that the URL is:

http://www.ora.com

In addition, you need to choose some text that will be displayed for this link, for example, "O'Reilly Web page." Using Table 10-2, we see that the link should look like:

```
<A HREF="http://www.ora.com">
O'Reilly Web page
</A>
```

This HTML is displayed as a familiar-looking link, labeled "O'Reilly Web page," ready to be selected.

STITCH YOUR HTML FILES TOGETHER

Once you are comfortable creating HTML files, you can combine them into a set of private Web pages, just as we did with the Web page construction program. Make some category files and a main file, put them into the same folder or directory, and make a bookmark for the main file.

QUIZ: Finding information again

1. What does your Web browser call the following?
   (a) Bookmarks
   (b) Your bookmark list

2. What kind of bookmark list does your browser support? Single? Multiple? Hierarchical?

3. All Web browsers let you add bookmarks, but what else does your browser let you do with them?
   (a) Rename them
   (b) Delete them
   (c) Reorder them
   (d) Sort them into alphabetical order
   (e) Change where they point (their URLs)
   (f) Add private comments about them
   (g) Anything else

4. Create a small set of private Web pages for your favorite links. You can either use a Web page construction program or write the HTML with a text editor. Pick three topics of interest, and for each one, make a page with a few links. Then make a main page that has links to your three topic pages.

Putting Information Online

11

This chapter explains how you can make a positive impact on the Net by contributing a little of yourself. We'll cover:

- Answering questions in a discussion group.
- Making and distributing an FAQ.
- Running a mailing list.
- Creating Web pages.
- Creating or moderating a newsgroup.

YOU ARE PART OF THE INTERNET

Chapter 3 explained that the Internet may be viewed as a huge library full of information on many topics. While this view has advantages, it is incomplete. In a public library, people may carry information out, but they generally don't put any back in, say, by writing books and donating them to the library. Instead, the library is a book-lending service.

On the Internet, consumption is only half the story. The Internet also thrives on active participation and contribution. Today's vast, worldwide repository of online information didn't appear by magic. It was created through the efforts of millions of users, many of them volunteers. They are perhaps the true "Internet community": the people who continue to build and maintain the multitude of resources on the Net.

Whether you are on the Internet for your business or yourself, you can be a part of this community and help the Internet grow. It's fun, satisfying, and even profitable. Your contribution can be as simple as answering questions about your favorite subject in a discussion group, or as complex as creating a Web site with dozens or hundreds of pages.

EARN THE PRAISE AND RESPECT OF YOUR PEERS

Have you ever wanted to be famous? The Net makes it possible. If you spend the time to create an information resource of good quality, you'll become known on the Net, at least among people who share your interests. Visibility on the Net can contribute to your business' reputation or publicize your company's expertise, as well as provide enjoyment for you. Contributing to a Net discussion can be like appearing on a panel at a trade show. Creating and maintaining a Web site can be like holding a seminar for interested parties.

"Who in the world has time for volunteer work?" you might ask. It's true that some contributions may be time-consuming, like managing a large Web site, but others can be produced by working only a few minutes a day, slowly building an information resource that eventually becomes impressive in size and scope.

"Why bother?" you also might ask. For starters, it's a good way to meet people who share your interests. They'll discover your information resource and send you email about it. You can also expect some publicity. As the maintainer of an information resource, some people will consider you an expert or at least knowledgeable about your subject. It's not uncommon to have your resource mentioned in a magazine or even to be contacted by the press.

Most of all, there's the good feeling that comes from giving of yourself—sharing your work and doing it well. Even if your contribution takes time, somehow it seems worthwhile when you receive email messages like this:

```
Hi—I just came across your Web site and wanted to let
you know that it is terrific! It's just what I was
looking for. You just saved me hours of work. If you
ever need a favor, just let me know. Thank you SO much!!
```

ANSWER QUESTIONS ABOUT YOUR FAVORITE TOPICS

The easiest way to make a contribution to the Internet is to participate in a discussion group, like a Usenet newsgroup or a local forum run by your online service provider. Locate one that focuses on your area of expertise or a favorite hobby, and join the discussion. When people post questions, take it upon yourself to answer them. After a while, other participants will come to know you and (assuming you give good answers) respect your opinion.

Back in 1990, just for fun, I started writing humorous articles on Usenet about computers. I wasn't looking for profit, just a creative outlet. A few years later, the articles caught the attention of *Compute* magazine, and they offered me a monthly column.	**Case Study: Volunteer work sometimes pays**

When the Web became popular, I decided to create a home page devoted to my favorite rock band, Gentle Giant. It had information about the band members, the albums, trivia, and other stuff. A year later, a major British magazine printed a picture of the Web page. This was exciting in itself, but it also caught the attention of PolyGram Records, who then hired me to assist in the production of a Gentle Giant CD anthology.

Volunteering on the Net is great. You never know where it will lead.

If your answers are of general interest, post them in the newsgroup for all to see. Otherwise, email your answers directly to the questioners.

Even if your responses expire after a few days—typical of Usenet news articles, for example—some sites collect these articles and make them available on the Web. Users in the future may locate your articles during a search and read your advice. So your words may have lasting value.

CREATE AN FAQ

If you notice that the users in a discussion group are asking the same questions repeatedly, consider making an FAQ, or Frequently Asked Questions document, to help them out. An FAQ contains the answers to common questions on a particular topic. Hundreds of FAQs are available on topics ranging from computer software to politics to body-piercing.

FAQs are tremendously helpful because they collect a lot of needed information as a single document. Writing one can be quite educational (and fun) because in the process, the writer learns a lot about the topic. The next section covers the ins and outs of creating an FAQ. Figure 11-1 illustrates what a typical FAQ looks like.

WRITE AN EFFECTIVE FAQ

In addition to choosing good questions and providing accurate answers, here are some tips for creating an FAQ masterpiece.

- *Solicit questions from others.* Even if you are an expert in your topic, it helps to get inspiration from other users, including novices. Post a note in a relevant newsgroup, announcing that you are preparing an FAQ and would like people to contribute questions and, if they wish, suggested answers. Alternatively, just use material that's been posted in the newsgroup (but always ask the authors' permission before including it in an FAQ).

  If your FAQ contains information you received from other people, it is polite to thank them in the FAQ. (Be sure to ask them first if they mind having their names or email addresses mentioned in the FAQ.) The easiest method is to add a "Special Thanks" section at the beginning or end of the document.

```
The Wombat FAQ
Prepared by Manny Mammal, mammal@wombat.com
```
Last date modified → `Last Updated: 30 May 1996`

```
ABOUT THIS FAQ
Wombat owners, unit! This FAQ answers questions
about keeping a wombat as a pet.

    The most recent version of this FAQ is
    posted on the first day of each month in
    rec.pets.wombats. It s also available on
    the World Wide Web at
    http://www.wombat.org/faq/. If you don t
    have Web or Usenet access, you can request
    the FAQ by email from mammal@wombat.org.

Please send comments or corrections to
mammal@wombat.org.
```

Category → `INDEX OF QUESTIONS`
```
A. General Questions
A.1 What is a wombat?
A.2 What do they look like?
```
Numbering scheme → `A.3 Why do wombats make good pets?`
```
B. Care and Feeding
B.1.1 My wombat seems allergic to nuts. What
should I do?
B.1.2 What is a good book on wombat allergies?
B.2 How often should wombats be bathed?
C. Competitions
C.1 What is the International Wombat
Competition(IWC)?
C.2. How do I enter my wombat in the IWC?
```

```
QUESTIONS AND ANSWERS
A. General Questions
A.1 What is a wombat?
Wombats are marsupials of the family
Vombatidae.
    Native to Australia, these furry creatures
    are often ...
```

FIGURE 11-1:
A sample FAQ

- *Organize questions into categories or subtopics.* Group related questions together, and write the name of the subtopic at the beginning of each group. For example, if your FAQ is about computers, you could make separate categories for software questions and hardware questions. Similarly, an FAQ about your favorite TV series could be partitioned into sections on characters, episode plots, the actors, and miscellaneous trivia.

- *Include an index of questions at the beginning of the FAQ.* This enables the reader to scan the questions quickly and determine whether the FAQ contains the information he or she wants to know.

- *Number the questions to aid searching.* Nowadays, most text-viewing programs allow users to search for desired information in a document. If you label each question with a unique number, a user can read the index, find the number of an interesting question, and quickly jump to the question by searching for its label.

  For this to work, the labels must be unique. You can either use consecutive numbers (1, 2, 3 ...) for the whole document, or you can number both the categories and the questions (e.g., questions in category A are labeled A.1, A.2 ..., and those in category B are labeled B.1, B.2 ..., etc.), like an outline. Figure 11-1 shows an example numbering scheme. Make sure, however, that you do not number your questions like this:

```
A. Category One
1. First question
2. Second question
B. Category Two
1. Another first question
2. Another second question
```

because the numbers are not unique. Both "First question" and "Another first question" are labeled "1," making searching less convenient. Instead, use a style that assigns each question a different label, like this:

```
A. Category One
A.1. First question
A.2. Second question
B. Category Two
B.1. Another first question
B.2. Another second question
```

- *Include contact information so people can send updates and corrections.* Include your real name, your email address, and the URL of your home page, if you have one.

- *Include the date that the FAQ was last updated.* An old version of a document can float around the Net for years, filled with obsolete information. Readers appreciate knowing the age of the information they're reading.

- *Describe how to obtain the latest version of the FAQ.* If the FAQ date is old, readers may want to locate the most recent edition of your FAQ. If possible, make your FAQ available on Usenet, on the Web, and by email.

- *Read other FAQs for more style ideas.* It's helpful to see how other people have organized their FAQs.

DISTRIBUTE YOUR FAQ

Usenet is a good medium for distributing your FAQ. Post it in a newsgroup devoted to the topic of your FAQ (or something closely relevant). Be sure to give it an informative subject line, such as:

```
Subject: Social Psychology Frequently Asked Questions
(FAQ)
```

so it can be recognized quickly by readers. Generic-looking subject lines like the following are unhelpful in comparison:

```
Subject: Psych FAQ
```

Consider posting your FAQ also in *news.answers*, a newsgroup devoted to FAQs of all kinds. *news.answers* is moderated. In order for your FAQ to be acceptable to the moderator, it must adhere to certain guidelines. These guidelines can be found on the Web at:

ftp://rtfm.mit.edu/pub/usenet/news.answers/news-answers/guidelines

or you can request them by sending an email message to *mail-server@rtfm.mit.edu* containing the line:

```
send usenet/news.answers/news-answers/guidelines
```

If your FAQ is accepted by *news.answers*, not only can you post it there, but also it will be automatically archived on the *news.answers* FTP site:

ftp://rtfm.mit.edu/pub/usenet/news.answers/

You can also make your FAQ into a Web page. We'll discuss this later in the chapter.

START A MAILING LIST

Mailing lists (Chapter 8) bring together a group of people with a common interest and provide them with a forum for holding discussions by email. Before creating a mailing list, make sure there isn't another one already devoted to your topic. Check the lists of mailing lists in Appendix A, as well as relevant FAQs and newsgroups.

Creating a mailing list often requires the help of your system administrator. Generally, all you'll need to provide is a name for the list. Keep the name short but descriptive. For example, if your mailing list is devoted to farm machinery, some reasonable names are *farm-machines* or *tractor-folks*, but *fm* would be bad.

Once the mailing list has been created, people may subscribe to it. Nowadays, most mailing list software handles subscriptions automatically. As shown in Chapter 8, new subscribers send email to a special address that adds them to the list. Older mailing list software, however, may require you to handle subscriptions manually, adding and removing subscribers who send requests to you. Ask your online service provider how it handles mailing list subscriptions.

It's a smart idea to create an introductory document to be mailed to new subscribers, explaining the purpose of the list and anything else you care to say. Some mailing list software will mail this document automatically whenever a user subscribes. In addition to welcoming the new subscriber, your document should explain:

- How to send a message to the list.
- How to send a message to you, the mailing list maintainer, in case of a problem.
- How to unsubscribe. (Don't forget this!)
- A reminder not to delete this document because it contains the important information above.

To publicize your mailing list, post an announcement in relevant Usenet newsgroups, and submit information about it to the various lists of mailing lists on the Net.

- Make a Web page about something you are truly interested in and knowledgeable about, something useful or entertaining to others. When I ran the NCSA "What's New" page, our staff saw 500 new sites a week. Some of our favorites were the Spam Haiku page (write your own), and the Twinkie experiments, where MIT students conducted very scientific lab experiments on Hostess Twinkies (measuring combustion rate, etc.) all with graphic photos. A funny site can be as great as a useful one. —Ellie Cutler

- Whenever you find a Web site that's been helpful to you, email the creator or maintainer so they know their site has been useful to someone else. —Fern Dickman

- Send money to the Free Software Foundation, Project GNU, or some similar undertaking that creates freely distributable software. —Kathleen Callaway

What other contributions can users make?

MAKE A WEB PAGE

Web pages are perhaps the most versatile and glamorous information resources on the Internet today. Whether you've got a few sentences or a multi-megabyte database to share, it seems that a Web page is the way to go.

In order to make a fancy Web page with links, graphics, and different text styles, you can either learn the Web page language, HTML, or use one of the many Web page construction programs available today. (Chapter 10 discusses HTML briefly, and explains how Web pages are created and posted on some major online service providers.) If you don't need the fancy features, however, you can put a plain text file on the Web—such as an FAQ—without any modifications. This can be done with any text editor or word processor, provided you save the file as "plain text" or "ASCII." Once this is done, before you can put your file on the Web, you need to find out:

- *Whether your online service provider allows users to have Web pages*: If not, you're out of luck unless you switch to a different online service provider.

- *Where to put your Web page file*: Do you need to move it to a particular directory or folder? Do you need to transfer it to another computer?

- *The URL of your page*, so you can tell others where to view it.

Promoting Your Web Site
http://www.best.com/ ~mentorms/eureka_i.htm

More information on promoting your Web site can be found here.

The answers to these questions vary from site to site. Consult your online service provider's system documentation, and if that doesn't help, ask their technical support staff.

ANNOUNCE YOUR WEB PAGE

Once you have created your wonderful Web page, there are several ways to tell the world about it.

- *Register your Web page with search engines.* Many search engines have a registration feature, as we discussed in Chapter 5, that adds your Web page to the search engine catalog. To register, visit the major search pages and look for a link for registering a new page or adding a URL.

  Active search engines, also discussed in Chapter 5, will likely locate your page automatically and add it to their catalogs.

  Companies have begun to emerge that, for a fee, will register your Web pages with all the major search engines. While this can save you time, be aware that similar services are becoming available on the Web for free. Several are listed at:

  http://www.best.com/~mentorms/e_howtms.htm

  http://www.yahoo.com/Computers_and_Internet/Internet/ World_Wide_Web/Announcement_Services/

- *Ask maintainers of related pages to add a link.* If you come across a Web page that has a topic related to yours, send the maintainer a polite note, asking if he or she will add a link pointing to your page. (It's polite for you also to add a link pointing to his or her page.) Don't go overboard with this method of announcement. If you send out too many requests, you may be accused of sending "junk email" and receive flames (nasty remarks).

- *Add your URL to your business card.* More and more people are including their home page URL on their cards, even for non-commercial Web pages.

- *Post an announcement on Usenet.* The moderated newsgroup *comp.infosystems.www.announce* is devoted to announcements of this type. Before you submit anything, however, read the newsgroup instructions. They are posted regularly in the newsgroup and are available on the Web at:

  http://boutell.com/~grant/charter.html

WebStep Top 100 Master Index
http://www.mmgco.com/ top100.html

This index suggests many free places to list your Web site.

Advertising online

Some advertisers seek to expand their customer base by flooding online discussion groups with advertisements. These advertisers don't participate in the ongoing discussions; all they do is post ads. In the process, they damage their reputations online. Who wants to buy from a company that interrupts people's discussions with impersonal, mass-market hype?

Internet users welcome commercial participation online as long as it contributes to the discussion. In technical newsgroups, for example, users love to receive advice from a vendor's technical support staff. They also appreciate seeing tasteful product announcements (i.e., lots of content and no marketing hype) posted in appropriate newsgroups, such as "announce" newsgroups on Usenet. This kind of Net-friendly participation is far more effective than using a discussion group as a dumping ground for ads.

As a businessperson, if you give of yourself freely in online discussions—answering questions, offering helpful tips, even cracking jokes—you'll earn the respect of the other regular participants. This, in turn, will lead to free publicity and a favorable reputation for your business. You might also get valuable feedback from appreciative users about your products and services.

In short, rather than treating the Internet like yet another advertising medium, think of it as a community to which you yourself belong. For more information, see the introductory documents in the Usenet newsgroup *news.announce.newusers*.

You might also post an announcement in a small number of relevant Usenet newsgroups. Don't post large numbers of duplicate announcements throughout Usenet. This is called spamming and may violate your online service provider's regulations. Ask your system administrator for the proper way to crosspost articles into multiple newsgroups from your account.

- *Read the World Wide Web FAQ.* Further tips for publicizing your Web page can be found in the World Wide Web FAQ by Thomas Boutell:

http://www.boutell.com/faq/pub.htm

MODERATE A NEWSGROUP

Some Usenet newsgroups have an official moderator who runs the newsgroup. Moderating a newsgroup can be a rewarding experience. As moderator, you set standards for the newsgroup, accept and reject articles, make minor edits, post articles that have been accepted, and possibly maintain an archive of posted articles, usually on a Web page or FTP site.

Being a moderator requires some technical expertise. One has to understand (or be willing to learn about) Usenet article headers, file compression, tar archives, Web page design, and FTP site maintenance.

There is no set method for becoming a newsgroup moderator. Usenet is very informal. Here are some ways that people have done it:

- *Create a new moderated newsgroup.* This is a lot of work, as we'll discuss in the next section.
- *Replace the moderator of an existing newsgroup.* Many moderators eventually retire from their positions, and when they do, they often post a note in their newsgroup (or other relevant newsgroups) looking for a replacement.

More information about moderating can be found at:

ftp://ftp.sterling.com/moderators/

Has volunteering paid off?

- More than I can list. I've met thousands of people online, many of whom later turned into personal friendships. I've gotten a lot of professional writing assignments from my online work and expertise. I've gotten tons of software products (and a bit of hardware and even books) sent to me for review. Manufacturers know that if I like something I'll be talking about it, and that will help spur their sales. —Harv Laser

- Oh, sure. Lots of new friends and fan mail. —Ellie Cutler

- Yes—I got to work on this book! —Fern Dickman

- I don't always enjoy maintaining my mailing lists and FTP sites. The enjoyable part happens when people use these resources to get together, work on a project, and share ideas. Maintaining the sites is just a necessary task in order to accomplish the rest. —Robert Strandh

CREATE A NEWSGROUP

Creating a Usenet newsgroup is a time-consuming task, but the results can be worth the effort. Briefly, the process is:

1. Write a proposed *charter* for the newsgroup, explaining its purpose and focus.

2. Start a public discussion about the pros and cons of creating the newsgroup.

3. If the newsgroup generally seems like a good idea, hold a vote by email.

4. If the vote passes, the newsgroup is created.

Each of these steps has further details explained in the document "How to Create a New Usenet Newsgroup," available on the Web at:

ftp://rtfm.mit.edu/pub/usenet/news.answers/usenet/creating-newsgroups/

Your online service provider might let you create a local newsgroup, forum, message board, etc., with a lot less effort. Ask your system administrator for more details.

THANK YOU

Thanks to the efforts of so many people who contribute their time, the Internet continues to grow and improve. New Web pages appear every few minutes. Search engines with more powerful capabilities are on the horizon. This is an exciting decade to be online.

I hope that the information in this book has been valuable to your search for knowledge and fun on the Net. For the latest information about this book, please check out the Web site:

http://www.ora.com/catalog/netresearch/

where I'll be posting updates and related materials.

Happy searching!

---

1. Locate an FAQ devoted to a topic that you like. Think of a question that isn't answered, answer it, and send both the question and the answer to the FAQ maintainer.	**QUIZ: Putting information online**

Appendix A: Great Places to Start a Search

It's hard to narrow down several million Web pages to produce a list of the so-called "best." So we didn't. Instead, we've listed some Web pages that are helpful in a general way. Rather than focusing on specific topics, these pages are designed to lead you to further information. For instance, instead of listing ten pages devoted to a topic, we list one page that points you to ten others.

Links to all of these pages can be found at:

http://www.ora.com/catalog/netresearch/

If any of these URLs go out of date, do a search for the title or topic of the page.

WEB SEARCH ENGINES

Lists of Search Engines

InterNIC	*http://www.internic.net/tools/*
Yahoo	*http://www.yahoo.com/Computers_and_ Internet/Internet/World_Wide_ Web/Searching_the_Web/*

All-In-One Search Pages

All-In-One Search Page	*http://www.albany.net/allinone/*
Search.Com	*http://www.search.com*

Search Engines, Active and Passive

AltaVista	*http://www.altavista.digital.com*
Excite	*http://www.excite.com*
HotBot	*http://www.hotbot.com*
InfoSeek	*http://www.infoseek.com*
Lycos	*http://www.lycos.com*
Magellan	*http://www.mckinley.com*
Open Text	*http://index.opentext.net*
WebCrawler	*http://www.webcrawler.com*
Yahoo	*http://www.yahoo.com*

Meta-Search Engines

Internet Sleuth	*http://www.isleuth.com*
MetaCrawler	*http://metacrawler.cs.washington.edu*
Net Locator	*http://nln.com*
SavvySearch	*http://guaraldi.cs.colostate.edu:2000/*
Starting Point	*http://www.stpt.com*

USENET SEARCH ENGINES

AltaVista	*http://www.altavista.digital.com*
Deja News	*http://www.dejanews.com*
Excite	*http://www.excite.com*

| InfoSeek | *http://www.infoseek.com* |
| Sift | *http://www.reference.com* |

GOPHER SEARCH ENGINES

Jughead	*gopher://gopher.utah.edu*
Veronica	*gopher://veronica.scs.unr.edu*
Yahoo	*http://www.yahoo.com/Computers_and_Internet/Internet/Gopher/Searching/*

FAQ ARCHIVES

Ohio State	*http://www.cis.ohio-state.edu/hypertext/faq/usenet/top.html*
Oxford	*http://www.lib.ox.ac.uk/internet/news/*
RTFM	*ftp://rtfm.mit.edu/pub/usenet-by-hierarchy/*

PEOPLE/ORGANIZATION SEARCH

Email Address Search

Four11	*http://www.four11.com*
NETFIND	*http://www.nova.edu/Inter-Links/netfind.html*
Who Where?	*http://www.whowhere.com*

Personal Home Page Lists

| Personal Pages Worldwide | *http://www.utexas.edu/world/personal/* |

Telephone Directories

BigYellow	*http://www.bigyellow.com*
InfoSpace	*http://www.infospace.com*
Lookup USA	*http://www.abii.com*
Switchboard	*http://www.switchboard.com*

| Who Where? | *http://www.whowhere.com* |
| Yahoo | *http://www.yahoo.com/search/people/* |

LISTS OF MAILING LISTS

Email Discussion Groups	*http://www.nova.edu/ Inter-Links/listserv.html*
List of Lists	*http://catalog.com/vivian/ interest-group-search.html*
Liszt	*http://www.liszt.com*
PAML	*http://www.neosoft.com/internet/paml/*
Tile.Net	*http://www.tile.net*

REFERENCE

Collections of Reference Materials

| Research-It! | *http://www.iTools.com/research-it/* |
| Yahoo Reference | *http://www.yahoo.com/Reference/* |

Specific Reference Materials

Area Codes	*http://www.555-1212.com/aclookup.html*
Bartlett's Quotations	*http://www.columbia.edu/ acis/bartleby/bartlett/*
Elements of Style	*http://www.columbia.edu/ acis/bartleby/strunk/*
CarlWeb (libraries)	*http://www.carl.org/carlweb/*
Roget's Thesaurus	*http://humanities.uchicago.edu/forms_ unrest/ROGET.html*
Unit converter	*http://www.webcom.com/legacysy/ convert2/convert2.html*
Vicinity (maps)	*http://infoseek.vicinity.com*
Webster's Dictionary	*http://civil.colorado.edu/htbin/dictionary*
Zip Codes	*http://www.usps.gov/ncsc/lookups /lookup_zip+4.html*

COMPUTERS AND INTERNET

Freely distributable software

Archie Services	*http://pubweb.nexor.co.uk/ public/archie/servers.html*
Jumbo	*http://www.jumbo.com*
Shareware.Com	*http://www.shareware.com*
Simtel	*http://www.simtel.net/archive/*
Software Sharing Resource Library	*http://ssrl.rtp.com:443*
ZD Net Software Library	*http://www.zdnet.com/zdi/software/*

Computer companies

Apple	*http://www.apple.com*
IBM	*http://www.ibm.com*
Microsoft	*http://www.microsoft.com*

Domain name directories

InterNIC (USA)	*http://www.internic.net/wp/whois.html*
InterNIC (USA)	*http://rs.internic.net/cgi-bin/whois*
JPNIC (Japan)	*http://www.nic.ad.jp/cgi-bin/whois_gate*
RIPE (Europe)	*http://www.ripe.net*
Yahoo (list)	*http://www.yahoo.com/Computers_and_ Internet/Internet/Directory_Services/*

U.S. GOVERNMENT RESOURCES

FedWorld	*http://www.fedworld.gov*
Internal Revenue Service	*http://www.irs.ustreas.gov*
Library of Congress	*http://www.loc.gov*
National Archives & Records Administration	*http://www.nara.gov*
Postal Service	*http://www.usps.gov*

Thomas (Congressional info)	http://thomas.loc.gov
White House	http://www.whitehouse.gov

SCIENCE

Ancient World Web	http://atlantic.evsc.virginia.edu/julia/AncientWorld.html
Discovery Channel	http://www.discovery.com
National Academy of Sciences	http://www.nas.edu

NEWS AND CURRENT EVENTS

CNN	http://cnn.com
New York Times	http://www.nytimes.com
Reuters	http://www.reuters.com
USA Today	http://www.usatoday.com
Wall St. Journal	http://wsj.com
Weather Channel	http://www.weather.com
Yahoo Weather	http://weather.yahoo.com

WHAT'S NEW/COOL ON THE NET?

comp.infosystems.www.announce	news:comp.infosystems.www.announce
Netscape What's New	http://home.netscape.com/home/whats-new.html
WebCrawler Top 25	http://www.webcrawler.com/WebCrawler/Top25.html
The Web 100	http://www.web100.com
Yahoo Picks	http://www.yahoo.com/picks/

BUSINESS

BanxQuote	*http://www.banx.com*
CompanyLink	*http://www.companylink.com*
Currency Converter	*http://www.xe.net/currency/*
Stock Quotes	*http://www.secapl.com/cgi-bin/qs*

ENTERTAINMENT

Music

Mammoth Music Meta-List	*http://www.vibe.com/mmm/*
Ultimate Band List	*http://ubl.com*

Art

1000 Points of Art	*http://members.aol.com/noahnet/art/*
World Wide Arts Resources	*http://wwar.world-arts-resources.com/*

Literature and Writing

On Line Books Page	*http://www.cs.cmu.edu/Web/books.html*
Project Bartleby	*http://www.cc.columbia.edu/acis/bartleby/*
Project Gutenberg	*http://www.promo.net/pg/*
Shakespeare Complete	*http://the-tech.mit.edu/Shakespeare/works.html*

Film

Internet Movie Database	*http://www.moviedatabase.com*
Movie Critic (recommendations)	*http://www.moviecritic.com*
Movie Review Query Engine	*http://www.cinema.pgh.pa.us/movie/reviews/*

Television

The Gist   *http://www.tv1.com*

Sports

Lycos Sports   *http://a2z.lycos.com/Sports/*

Yahoo Sports   *http://www.yahoo.com/Recreation/Sports/*

Appendix B: Answers to Quiz Questions

CHAPTER 1

1. It's likely that you got far more results than you need, and possibly many irrelevant ones. Don't worry—we'll learn how to narrow our searches later.

2. Most likely, both Yahoo and InfoSeek found something on your topics, even if it isn't quite what you're looking for. Yahoo is what's called a "passive" search engine, and InfoSeek is an "active" search engine—we'll learn the difference in Chapter 5.

3. Hope to see you there!

4. Don't stay up too late.

CHAPTER 2

1. If you use an online service provider mentioned at the end of the chapter, try the methods found in the section "Commercial online service providers have resources." Try searching for words like `Internet`, `Web`, `FTP`, `email`, `mail`, `electronic mail`, and so on.

2. Use your Web browser to do this.

3. Use your Web browser to do this.

4. Use your Web browser to do this.

5. *news.announce.newusers* contains informative (and sometimes hu-

morous) articles about Usenet, written especially for new users. If your online service provider doesn't supply a newsreader, skip to the next question.

6. If this doesn't work, either your online service provider doesn't have access to Usenet, or your Web browser doesn't support Usenet URLs. Ask a technical support person for assistance.

7. Hello to you too!

CHAPTER 3

1. You might also ask some colleagues to describe the Internet and see how their views compare with those presented in this chapter.

2. This question doesn't have a unique "correct" answer. My opinions are:

   (a) *Resource view*. Look for an online stock price service.

   (b) *Program view*. Since you already know this is a Usenet newsgroup, use a newsreader to locate it.

   (c) *Library view*. Look up `united states president` using a Web search engine.

   (d) *Resource view*. Look for an Internet movie review database.

   (e) *Computer view*. We've given the URL for Yahoo several times, so connect to it directly.

3. Viewing the Internet as a community is helpful for searching because there are many knowledgeable people online. No matter what your question is, someone out there probably knows the answer or can tell you where to look for it.

   This view has disadvantages, however. Imagine what would happen if users posted public questions every time they needed help. The number of posted articles would increase drastically, making it difficult for other newsgroup participants to conduct conversations. In other words, when people post public questions, they add a small burden to the rest of the participants. This is why it's best to try other search techniques before posting public questions.

   Chapter 8 is devoted to helping you locate online communities that match your interests, where you can find friends for trading tips, experts to help you out, and novices *you* can help out.

4. How about a view that the Internet is a community of editors? Each person on the Net has likes and dislikes. People communicate their opinions in posted articles, on their home pages, and so on. As you become familiar with a particular person's opinions, you can use them as a shortcut to information. For instance, if someone posts a lot of articles about woodworking, you may discover that his/her home page is filled with woodworking tips. If someone writes lots of movie reviews online, check some of his/her reviews of movies you've already seen; if you agree with the reviews, read the newer ones to find movies you might like to see next.

CHAPTER 4

1. Some issues to think about are: ease of use, speed, relevance of the information they find, layout of the search page, good use of graphics (too many pictures means a long download time), and documentation.

2. (a) *sci.physics*

   (b) *rec.aquaria.misc*

   (c) *rec.games.video*

   (d) *misc.jobs*

   (e) Could be anything!

   (f) One of the many *soc.religion* or *alt.religion* newsgroups, as well as *soc.atheism*.

3. Try searching for `investment FAQ`. While you're connected to Deja News, search for other topics of interest and experiment with the various features. It's quite a powerful resource.

4. Asking a knowledgeable colleague is helpful because it might relieve you from having to search. On the other hand, it requires interrupting someone else's day, and you might have to wait a long time for an answer when you could have found it yourself.

5. The Web site of a public library can help you look up books on whatever topics you need. Connect to a search engine and try to find some libraries with online catalogs.

CHAPTER 5

1. If you can't find the information, consider sending email to the user *webmaster* at that site. (There may be a link on the main Web page for sending mail to this person.) Be aware that not everybody uses the terms "active" and "passive," so you might need to rephrase the question as something like, "How does your search engine build its catalog: with a spider? By having users register their pages?"

2. Again, if you can't find this information, ask the *webmaster*.

3. Look on the advanced query page, if there is one. Sometimes a link labeled Customize or Options will lead you in the right direction. Remember that not all operators are typed; sometimes they are selected from a list on the page, or appear as on/off buttons.

4. Try searching for the name of the vacation spot. If you don't get good results, try an advanced query.

5. Try searching for the name of the illness. On Yahoo, follow the Health link followed by Diseases and Conditions. (These names may change.)

6. It may be helpful to enclose the person's full name in quotes (or whatever the equivalent is for that search engine) so the full name is matched, not just the first or last name.

7. To determine this, do a search for anything. Does the page of results also have a search facility? Is your query already loaded and ready to be edited?

8. If the location has changed, do a Yahoo (or other) search for `"all in one search page"` (with the quotes).

9. Meta-search engines send your query to multiple search engines simultaneously. All-in-one search engines don't; they just provide a convenient user interface for querying many search engines, one at a time.

10. If this URL is obsolete, do a Web search for `veronica AND gopher`.

CHAPTER 6

1. (a) *apple.com*

   (b) *wbr.com* is one of 70 domain names registered by Warner Brothers.

   (c) *swarthmore.edu*

   (d) *rit.edu*

2. (a) *http://www.microsoft.com*

   (b) *http://www.cs.stanford.edu*

   (c) *http://www.fbi.gov*

   (d) *http://www.towerrecords.com*

   (e) *http://www.greenpeace.org*

3. See "Domain Name Directories" in Appendix A.

4. For example, for Windows 95, open an MS-DOS window and type:

   `tracert www.yahoo.com`

   `tracert www.altavista.digital.com`

   When querying the InterNIC for these two sites, ask for information on *yahoo.com* and *digital.com*. Always give the "domain name" (the last two words of the computer name).

5. As above, type:

   `tracert` *some.computer.in.the.world*

   for whatever computer you choose.

CHAPTER 7

1. Remember to enclose the person's full name in quotes (if supported by the search engine you use) and to try nicknames.

2. See "Telephone Directories" in Appendix A.

3. Some features might be: free access; looking up a name, given the phone number; looking up both people and businesses; and a responsible privacy policy.

4. See "Telephone Directories" and "Email Address Search" in Ap-

pendix A.

5. Search for the person's name and/or email address. If an email address is found, you'll be shown a list of newsgroups in which he/she has posted. Pretty neat.

6. There are a bunch at *http://www.yahoo.com/Arts/Humanities/ History/Genealogy/*.

CHAPTER 8

1. See "Lists of Mailing Lists" in Appendix A.

2. If you don't find one in any of the lists of mailing lists, check the FAQ of a related Usenet newsgroup. (Search for a related newsgroup using a newsreader and the instructions in Chapter 4 .)

3. Which provided faster or more accurate results: the list of mailing lists, or the Web search?

4. Try it by several different methods to see which is quickest.

5. Use the instructions in Chapter 4 for searching for Usenet newsgroup names. Or try the Usenet Info Center.

6. Use the methods in Chapter 1 in the section "Commercial online service providers have resources." Search for `mailing list`.

7. Same as the previous answer, but search for `chat`. If you can't find anything by searching for chat groups, try searching for topics of interest. Perhaps related chat groups will be accessible nearby.

8. Same as the previous answer, but search for `IRC` or `Internet Relay Chat`.

CHAPTER 9

1. Use the newsgroup table in this chapter as a guide. To find a newsgroup, use the instructions in Chapter 4 for searching for Usenet newsgroup names. Or try the Usenet Info Center.

2. Go to *www.shareware.com* and search for `virus` or `virus checker`.

3. Search for `"word processor"` AND `"windows 95"` AND

```
shareware.
```

4. Search for (screensaver OR "screen saver") AND (mac OR macintosh) AND freeware.

5. Search for "atomic clock".

6. Search for the name or the archiver. Don't do an Archie search for this because many archive files will have the archiver name as part of the filename. For example, every Zip file has a name ending in zip, so searching for zip will produce huge numbers of irrelevant hits.

   Don't be satisfied with the first hit you find. Old versions of the program could still be documented online. Look for an "official" site devoted to the program, ideally, a site maintained by the author or distributor.

7. Do a Web search or "people" search for the author. Don't forget to check your favorite program's documentation—the information might be there.

8. Do a search for the type of the program.

CHAPTER 10

1. (a) Bookmarks? Shortcuts? Favorites? Hotlinks?

   (b) Hotlist? Bookmark list? Favorites?

2. If you see folders in your bookmark list, it's probably hierarchical. Otherwise, look for just one bookmark list or many.

3. Once you find out, create some bookmarks and practice using the commands. Good bookmark management is a handy skill.

4. If possible, use a Web page construction program; it's less trouble.

CHAPTER 11

1. Try it!

Index

academic papers, searching for, 73, 130
access time, speeding up, 62, 63
accuracy of information, 6-8
active search engines, 51, 52
addresses, postal
  finding, 96
advanced queries, 57-60
advertising
  in newsgroups, 161
  Web sites, 6-8
all-in-one search pages, 74, 166
AltaVista, 38, 69, 140
  Usenet searches, 46
Alternic, 79
America Online
  chat groups, 115
  connecting to URLs, 12
  connecting to Web, 3
  downloading software, 121
  Find command, 18
  finding members, 98
  finding newsgroup names, 44
  message boards, 113
  Personal Publisher, 144
  searching, 18
  Web page construction, 144
anonymous FTP, 126-28
Archie, 128, 130
archivers, 130-31
auto-responders, 17

Back button, 62
"A Beginner's Guide to URLs", 29
BinHex, 131
bookmarks, 134-36
  compared to copying Web pages, 134-36
  organizing, 136-37

  private Web pages for, 141, 144-47, 150
  shortcomings, 140
  stale, 137-39
  for subpages, 138-39
Boolean operators. See operators
Boutell, Thomas, 161
"A Brief Guide to Social Newsgroups and Mailing Lists", 112
browsers. See Web browsers
business Web sites, 171

Callaway, Kathleen, 39, 46, 51, 54, 67, 70, 94, 108, 137, 141, 159
case studies
  ballroom dancing, mailing list, 111
  book review, outdated link, 140
  graphics cards, 70
  locating people, 94, 97
  recipes, 46
  stock prices, 51
  volunteer work, 153
catalogs, of search engines, 50, 51-55, 70
categories, searching by, 70
channels, 116
charters, of newsgroups, 163
chat groups, 113-16
  finding, 115-16
  IRC (Internet Relay Chat), 115, 116
  on online services, 115
  Web pages for, 115
citations for online resources, 142
colleges and universities
  alumni search services, 104
  department names, 83-84
commercial online services. See online service providers

community, Internet as, 152
compressed files, 130-31
CompuServe
    chat groups, 115
    connecting to URLs, 12
    connecting to Web, 3
    Directory, 18
    downloading software, 121
    finding members, 98
    finding newsgroup names, 44
    forums, 113
    Home Page Wizard, 144
    searching, 18
    Web page construction, 144
computer names, 24-25, 76
    in academic departments, 83-84
    guessing, 25, 81-86
    subdomains in, 80-81
    understanding, 80
    in URLs, 77
computers
    hops between, 87, 88-89
    finding, 76
    Internet viewed as collection of,
        23-25
    network locations, 87
    newsgroups devoted to, 123-24
    physical locations, 25, 87
    upgrading, 63
    user groups, 124
contributions, to Internet,
    152-53, 159
copyright issues, 136
country codes, 78-79
crawlers, 51
Cutler, Ellie, 11, 16, 34, 39, 51, 54,
    67, 70, 94, 108, 111, 137, 159,
    162

da Silva, Stephanie, 111
databases, of search engines.
    See catalogs
dearchivers, 130
Deja News, 46, 98
demoware, 121
Dickman, Fern, 11, 34, 39, 51, 94,
    137, 141, 159, 162
digest form, of mailing lists, 112
directories
    email addresses, 93-95
    online services, 18
    See also search engines
discussion groups, 14-15, 113
    asking questions in, 43

participating in, 153-54
    See also Usenet news
distance between computers, 25
domains, 77-79
    country codes, 78-79
    searching for, 86, 169
    sub-, 79, 80-81
    top-level, 77-79
downloading
    files, 13, 125-27, 128, 129
    software, 120-22, 125-26
    See also FTP

educational institutions.
    See colleges and universities
"EFF's (Extended) Guide to the
    Internet", 18
electronic mailboxes, 17
Emacs GNUS, 44
email, 16-17
    to experts, 43
    postmasters, 103
    programs, 16-17, 26
    reading, 17
    See also mailing lists
email addresses, 16-17
    auto-responding, 17
    changed, 102-3
    directories, 93-95
    finding, 92, 93-95, 97-100, 167
    guessing, 100-102
    of mailing lists, 109
    standard forms, 101, 102
    URLs for, 29-30, 142
    usernames in, 101, 102
    verifying, 99-100
    of Web site maintainers, 6-7
Eureka Search Engine, 52
Excite, 38, 69

failed searches, 3-5, 67
FAQs (Frequently Asked
    Questions), 41-42
    archivers, 167
    consulting, 42
    creating, 154-57
    distributing, 157-58
    finding, 41, 46, 124
    about FTP, 13
    about Internet Relay Chat, 116
    organization, 156
    posted on Usenet, 42, 124,
        157-58

on Web pages, 159
    about World Wide Web,
        10, 161
favorites. See bookmarks
files
    archives, 130-31
    compressed, 130-31
    downloading, 13-14, 125-27,
        128, 129
    paths, 143
    searching for, 128, 130
    uploading, 13-14, 127
    URLs for local, 29, 142-43
finger program, 98, 99, 101
forums. See discussion groups
Four11, 93-94, 96
fraud, 8
Free Agent, 44
freely distributable software. See
    software
freeware, 121
    See also software
Frequently Asked Questions. See
    FAQs
friends. See people, finding
FTP (File Transfer Protocol), 13-14
    anonymous, 126-28
    commands, 127-28, 129
    downloading files, 125-27,
        128, 129
    FAQ, 13
    graphical user interface, 127
    searching for files, 128, 130
    sites, 13-14
    uploading files, 127
    URLs, 29, 142

genealogy, 105
general searches, 64, 65-66
GNU General Public License (GPL)
    software, 121
GNUS, 44
Gopher, 13
    search engines, 73, 167
    URLs, 29-30, 142
Gopher Jewels, 13
GPL (GNU General Public License)
    software, 121
graphics, turning off, 62
Gravity, 44
guessing, 40-41
    computer names, 25, 81-86
    domain names, 82-84
    email addresses, 100-102

home pages of individuals, 103-4
   URLs, 81-86, 103-4
gzip, 130

hard drives
   sizes, 63
   URLs for files on, 29, 142-43
   Web pages on, 62, 134-36
hardware, upgrading, 63
Hippie, 145
"The History of the Internet", 17
hits, 51
   number displayed, 68-69
   ranking, 71-72
home pages, 62
   See also Web pages; Web sites
Home Page Wizard, 144
HopCheck, 88
hops, 87, 88-89
HotBot, 38, 69
hotlinks. See bookmarks
hotlist items. See bookmarks
.hqx files, 131
HTML (HyperText Markup Language), 147
   creating links, 149-50
   learning, 147
   tags, 147-48
http (HyperText Transfer Protocol), 29
   omitting from URLs, 85
   See also URLs

images. See graphics
incremental searches, 66-67
indexes, of search engines.
   See catalogs
individuals. See people
InfoSeek, 38, 69
interleaved conversations, 114
Internet Address Finder, 94
Internet Explorer. See Microsoft Internet Explorer
InterNIC, 86, 95
IRC (Internet Relay Chat), 115, 116

Jughead servers, 73

keywords, 31, 50
   choosing, 55-56
   substring searches, 67-68

Laser, Harv, 16, 34, 46, 51, 54, 59, 67, 70, 94, 108, 111, 137, 141, 162
lha, 130
library, Internet viewed as, 30-33
links, 3
   creating, 149-50
   following, 3, 10-11
   URLs, 29
List of WWW Archie Services, 128
live chat. See chat groups
locations, of computers
   geographic, 25, 87
   network, 87
Lycos, 38, 69
lynx, 12, 62, 69

MacTraceroute, 88
Magellan, 38, 69
mailing lists, 108
   addresses, 109
   advantages and disadvantages, 108, 116-17
   digests, 112
   introductory documents, 110, 158
   lists of, 111, 168
   maintainers, 109
   members, 108
   netiquette, 110
   starting, 158
   subscribing, 108, 109-10, 158
   unsubscribing, 108, 110
   See also email
maintainers, of mailing lists, 109
matches. See hits
message boards. See discussion groups
MetaCrawler, 40
meta-search engines, 39-40, 52, 54, 166
Microsoft Internet Explorer
   bookmark management, 137
   connecting to URLs, 12
Microsoft Network (MSN)
   chat groups, 115
   connecting to Web, 3
   downloading software, 121
   finding members, 98
   finding newsgroup names, 44
   forums, 113
   personal Web pages, 145
   searching, 18
Microsoft News, 44

mirror sites, 88
modems, speeds, 63
moderating newsgroups, 162
Mosaic, connecting to URLs, 12

navigating Web, 10-11
   See also links
NCSA Mosaic, connecting to URLs, 29
net.citizen Directory Service, 94
netiquette, 113
   advertising, 161
   on mailing lists, 110
netnews. See Usenet news
Netscape Navigator
   bookmarks, 136
   connecting to URLs, 12, 85
Netscape News, 44
Netscape SmartMarks, 136
news. See Usenet news
news.answers, 157
newsgroups, 14-15
   local, 113
   names, 15
   See also Usenet news
newsreaders, 15, 27, 43-46
nicknames, 114-115
nn newsreader, 45

OKRA net.citizen Directory Service, 94
online service providers
   chat groups, 115
   connecting to URLs, 12
   connecting to Web, 3
   discussion groups, 14-15, 43, 113, 153-54
   downloading software, 121
   finding members, 98
   searching, 18
   Web page construction, 144-45
   See also specific providers
Open Text, 38, 69
operating systems, newsgroups devoted to, 123-24
operators, 50, 57-59, 60
   default, 61
   precedence, 65-66
organization of Internet, 22-23

PAML (Publicly Accessible Mailing Lists), 111
Parker, Bob, 16, 54, 59, 108

passive search engines, 51-52, 54-55
paths, file, 143
people, finding, 91-106
  addresses, 96
  case studies, 94, 97
  email addresses, 92, 93-95, 97-100, 167
  genealogy resources, 105
  guessing email addresses, 100-102
  not connected to Internet, 104-5
  on online services, 98
  privacy issues, 92, 96
  software authors, 125
  starting points, 167-68
  telephone numbers, 96, 167-68
  on Usenet, 97-98, 104-5
  Web pages, 92-93, 103-4, 167
  white pages services, 93-94, 96-97, 167-68
  x.500 directories, 95
Personal Publisher, 144
PKZIP, 130
posting, 15
postmasters, 103
precedence, of operators, 65-66
priority score of hits, 71
privacy issues, 92, 96
Prodigy
  chat groups, 115
  connecting to URLs, 12
  connecting to Web, 3
  downloading software, 121
  finding members, 98
  finding newsgroup names, 45
  Hippie, 145
  interest groups, 113
  searching, 18
  Web page construction, 145
programs
  archivers, 130
  BinHex, 131
  dearchivers, 130
  email, 16-17
  finger, 98, 99, 101
  Free Agent, 44
  Gravity, 44
  grip, 130-31
  Hippie, 145
  Home Page Wizard, 144
  hopCheck, 88
  lha, 130-31

Internet viewed as collection of, 25-27
learning, 26-27
lynx, 12, 62, 69
MacTraceroute, 88
Microsoft Internet Explorer, 10, 12
Microsoft News, 44
Netscape Navigator, 10, 12, 85
Netscape News, 44
newsreaders, 15, 27, 43-46
nn, 45
Personal Publisher, 144
PKZIP, 130
rn, 45
SmarkMarks, 136
Stuffit Expander, 130
tar, 130-31
tin, 45
traceroute, 88-89
tracert, 88
trn, 45
Trumpet, 45
uncompress, 130
virus checking, 120
vrfy, 99-100
Web page construction, 144-45
WhatRoute, 88
WinZip, 130
xrn, 45
  See also software; Web browsers
public domain software, 121
  See also software
Publicly Accessible Mailing Lists (PAML), 111

queries, 31, 50-51
  advanced, 57-59, 60
  choosing keywords, 55-56
  hits, 51, 68-69
  operators, 50, 57-59, 60, 61
  ranking hits, 71-72
  search strategies, 62-72
  simple, 55, 56-57, 61
query languages, 59, 61

RAM, adding, 63
ranks, of hits, 71-72
refinding information, 133
registering, with search engines, 52, 160
resources, Internet viewed as collection of, 27-30
rn newsreader, 45
robots, 51

Rosencrantz, Michael, 59
rtfm.mit.edu, 124
Rules for the Road, 5
SavvySearch, 40
Schneider, Dan, 105
.sea files, 131
search-and-jump, 68-69
search-and-rank, 71-72
search engines, 2, 38-39, 166
  active, 51, 52
  catalogs, 50, 51-55, 70
  categories, 70
  documentation on, 57, 61
  learning multiple, 27
  meta-, 39-40, 52, 54, 166
  number of hits displayed, 68-69
  operator precedence, 65-66
  passive, 51-52, 54-55
  query languages, 59, 61
  ranking techniques, 71-72
  registering Web sites with, 52, 160
  shortcomings, 54
  for software, 121-22
  specialized, 40
  Usenet, 45-46, 97-98, 166-67
  using, 31-32
  See also queries
searches
  for academic papers, 73, 130
  by category, 70
  example, 2-3
  failures, 3-5, 67
  for freely distributable software, 120, 121-25
  for FTP files, 128, 130
  general, 64, 65-66
  Gopher, 73, 167
  incremental, 66-67
  of online service providers, 18
  Rules for the Road, 5
  specific, 64-66
  speeding up, 62, 63
  starting points, 37, 46-47
  strategies, 62-72
  for text in Web pages, 68-70
  of Usenet news, 16, 45-46
  See also people, finding; queries
Search the Net in Style, 38
search strings. See queries
search terms. See keywords
shareware, 121-22
  See also software

simple queries, 55, 56-57
    default operators, 61
SmartMarks, 136
soc.net-people, 105
software
    archive formats, 130-31
    authors, 125
    checking for viruses, 120
    demos, 121
    downloading from online
        services, 121
    downloading with FTP, 125-27
    finding, 120, 121-25, 169
    freely distributable, 120, 121
    See also programs
specific searches, 64-66
spiders, 51
stale links, 137
Stop button, 63
Strandh, Robert, 16, 39, 51, 67, 70,
    111, 137, 141, 162
strategies for searching
    general searches, 64, 65-66
    incremental searches, 66-67
    search-and-jump, 68-69
    search-and-rank, 71-72
    searches by category, 70
    specific searches, 64-66
    substring searches, 67-68
Stuffit Expander, 130
subdomains, 79, 80-81
subscribing, to mailing lists, 108,
    109-10, 158
substring searches, 67-68
Switchboard, 96

tags (HTML), 147-48
tar, 130
Taylor, Dave, 112
telephone numbers, finding, 96
telnet, 30
text-based Web browsers, 62, 69
Timar, Cary, 105
tin newsreader, 45
top-level domains, 77-79
traceroute programs, 88-89
transmissions
    hops, 87, 88-89
    speed, 87-88
trn newsreader, 45
Trumpet, 45

uncompress, 130
universities. See colleges and
    universities
UNIX machines
    finding users, 98
    Web page construction, 145
unsubscribing, from mailing lists,
    108, 110
uploading files, 13,-14 127
    See also FTP
URLs (Uniform Resource Locators),
    11-12, 29-30
    citing, 142
    computer names in, 77
    for email, 29-30, 142
    for FTP sites, 29-30, 142
    for Gopher sites, 29-30, 142
    guessing, 81-86, 103-4
    for local files, 29, 142-43
    for newsgroups, 29-30, 85, 142
    outdated, 137-40, 141
    parts of, 29
    types of, 29, 30, 142
    typing in, 2, 12
    See also bookmarks
Usenet Addresses Service, 98
Usenet Info Center, 14, 43, 112
Usenet news, 14-16
    advantages and disadvantages,
        116-117
    advertising in, 161
    announcing Web sites on,
        160-61
    asking questions on, 43
    charters, 163
    creating newsgroups, 163
    FAQs posted on, 42, 124, 157-58
    finding email addresses in, 97-98
    finding newsgroups, 43-45, 112
    finding people, 104-5
    location, 85
    moderating, 162
    newsreaders, 15, 27
    participating in, 153-54
    postings, 15
    searching, 16, 45-46, 97-98,
        166-67
    on specific computers and
        operating systems, 123-24
    URLs, 29-30, 85, 142
    See also newsgroups
User groups, 124
usernames, in email addresses,
    101, 102

Venkataraman, Sridhar, 105
Veronica servers, 73
views of Internet, 21-22
    changing, 22, 33-34
    computer view, 23-25
    program view, 25-27
    resource view, 27-30
    as community, 152
    library view, 30-33
virus checking programs, 120
volunteering, 153-54, 162
vrfy program, 99-100

wanderers, 51
Wassenaar, Eric, 99
Web. See World Wide Web
Web browsers
    Back button, 62
    bookmark management, 136-37
    Find feature, 68-70
    learning, 26
    speeding up, 62, 63
    Stop button, 63
    text-based, 62, 69
    turning off graphics, 62
    typing in URLs, 2
    URL-guessing feature, 85
WebCrawler, 38, 69
Web pages, 10-11
    for bookmarks, 141, 144-47
    for chat groups, 115
    construction programs, 144-45
    creating, 144-50, 159-60
    on hard drive, 62, 134-36
    of individuals, 92-93, 103-4,
        167
    links, 3, 10-11
    private, 141, 144-47, 150
    searching for text in, 68-70
    for this book, 163
    See also bookmarks; HTML
Web search engines. See search
engines
Web sites
    email address of maintainer, 6-7
    errors on, 6-7
    finding, 92-93, 103-4
    finding sites that have moved,
        137-40, 141
    mirror sites, 88
    promoting, 159, 160-61
    registering with search engines,
        52, 160

software collection indexes, 122
specialized, 40
WhatRoute, 88
white pages services, 93-94, 96-97, 167-68
whois database, 86, 95
whois services, 87
Who Where, 96
WinZip, 130
wombats, 155

World Wide Web, 10
connecting to from online services, 3
FAQ, 10, 161
navigating, 10-11
See also Web sites

X.500 directory service, 95
xrn newsreader, 45

Yahoo, 2, 22-23, 38, 54-55, 69, 125
Yellow Pages, Internet, 27-28

.Z files, 131
.zip files, 131

More Titles from O'Reilly

Songline Guides

NetLearning: Why Teachers Use the Internet

By Ferdi Serim & Melissa Koch
1st Edition June 1996
304 pages, ISBN 1-56592-201-8

In this book educators and Internet users who've been exploring its potential for education share stories to help teachers use this medium to its fullest potential in their classrooms. The book offers advice on how to adapt, how to get what you want, and where to go to get help. The goal: To invite educators online with the reassurance there will be people there to greet them. Includes CD-ROM with Internet software.

NetSuccess: How Real Estate Agents Use the Internet

By Scott Kersnar
1st Edition August 1996
214 pages, ISBN 1-56592-213-1

This book shows real estate agents how to harness the communications and marketing tools of the Internet to enhance their careers and make the Internet work for them. Through agents' stories and "A day in the life" scenarios, readers see what changes and what stays the same when you make technology a full partner in your working life.

NetActivism: How Citizens Use the Internet

By Ed Schwartz
1st Edition September 1996
224 pages, ISBN 1-56592-160-7

Let a veteran political activist tell you how to use online networks to further your cause. Whether you are a community activist, a politician, a nonprofit staff person, or just someone who cares about your community, you will benefit from the insights this book offers on how to make the fastest-growing medium today work for you. Includes CD-ROM with Internet software and limited free online time.

NetResearch: Finding Information Online

By Daniel J. Barrett
1st Edition Winter 1997
240 pages (est.), ISBN 1-56592-245-X

Whatever your profession or avocation, NetResearch will show you how to locate the information in the constantly changing online world. Whether you're research statistics for a report, to find free software, or to locate an old college roommate, it pays to locate online information rapidly. But the Net is a very big, disorganized place, and it can be difficult to locate just the information you want, when you need it. In NetResearch, you'll learn effective search techniques that work with any Internet search programs. The author offers quizzes that allow you to practice your own research skills or that you can use as a teaching tool to help others. Covers the Internet, America Online, CompuServe, Microsoft Network, and Prodigy.

NetTravel: How Travelers Use the Internet

By Michael Shapiro
1st Edition Winter 1997
225 pages (est.), ISBN 1-56592-172-0

NetTravel is a virtual toolbox of advice for those travelers who want to tap into the rich vein of travel resources on the Internet. It is filled with personal accounts by travelers who've used the Net to plan their business trips, vacations, honeymoons, and explorations. Author and journalist Michael Shapiro gives readers all the tools they need to use the Net immediately to find and save money on airline tickets, accommodations, and car rentals. Includes CD-ROM with Internet software.

Net Law: How Lawyers Use the Internet

By Paul Jacobsen
1st Edition Winter 1997
254 pages (est.), ISBN 1-56592-258-1

From simple email to sophisticated online marketing, Net Law shows how the solo practitioner or the large law firm can turn the Net into an effective and efficient tool. Through stories from those who've set up pioneering legal Net sites, attorney Paul Jacobsen explains how lawyers can successfully integrate the Internet into their practices, sharing lessons "early adoptees" have learned. Includes CD-ROM with Internet software and limited free online time.

O'REILLY™

Software

WebSite™ 1.1

By O'Reilly & Associates, Inc.
Documentation by Susan Peck & Stephen Arrants
2nd Edition January 1996
Four diskettes, 494-pg book, WebSite T-shirt
ISBN 1-56592-173-9; UPC 9-781565-921733

 *WebSite 1.1* makes it easier than ever for Windows NT 3.51 and Windows 95 users to start publishing on the Internet. WebSite is a 32-bit multi- threaded World Wide Web server that combines power and flexibility with ease of use. *WebSite 1.1* features include: HTML editor, multiple indexes, WebFind wizard, CGI with Visual Basic 4 framework and server push support, graphical interface for creating virtual servers, Windows 95 style install, logging reports for individual documents, HTML-2 and -3 support, external image map support, and Spyglass Mosaic 2.1 Web browser.

WebSite Professional ™

By O'Reilly & Associates, Inc.
Documentation by Susan Peck
1st Edition June 1996
Includes 3 books, ISBN 1-56592-174-7

 Designed for the sophisticated user, *WebSite Professional™* is a complete Web server solution. *WebSite Professional* contains all of *WebSite*'s award-winning features, including remote administration, virtual servers for creating multiple home pages, wizards to automate common tasks, a search tool for Web indexing, and a graphical outline fo Web documents and links for managing your site. New with *WebSite Professional:* support for SSL and S-HTTP, the premier Web encryption security protocols; the WebSite Application Programming Interface (WSAPI); Cold Fusion, a powerful development tool for dynamic linking of database information into your Web documents; and support for client and server-side Java programming.

WebSite Professional is a must for sophisticated users who want to offer their audiences the best in Web server technology.

WebBoard ™

By O'Reilly & Associates, Inc.
1st Edition February 1996
Includes 3 diskettes & a 98-pg book, ISBN 1-56592-181-X

 *WebBoard™* is an advanced multi-threaded conferencing system that can help attract users to your Web server. With *WebBoard,* people can use their Web browsers to participate in online discussions about any number of topics. *WebBoard* is ideal for use in business environments and in legal or educational organizations or groups—anywhere online discussions can help groups communicate and keep track of ongoing decisions and issues.

PolyForm™

Documentation by John Robert Boynton
1st Edition May 1996
Two diskettes & 146-pg book, ISBN 1-56592-182-8

 *PolyForm™* is a powerful 32-bit Web forms tool that helps you easily build and manage interactive Web pages. *PolyForm*'s interactive forms make it easy and fun for users to respond to the contents of your Web with their own feedback, ideas, or requests for more information. *PolyForm* lets you collect, process, and respond to each user's specific input. Best of all, forms that once required hours of complicated programming can be created in minutes because *PolyForm* automatically handles all of the CGI programming for processing form contents.

Statisphere™

By O'Reilly & Associates, Inc.
1st Edition Winter 1996
2 diskettes & a 135-page book, ISBN 1-56592-233-6

 *Statisphere™* is a Web traffic analyzer that provides precise, graphical reporting on your Web server's usage. Easy-to-read, browser-based reports deliver real-time profiles and long-term trend analysis on who's visiting your site and what they're reading. Whether you're tracking traffic rates for advertising, or steering Web development efforts to where they'll have the most impact, Statisphere gives you the answers you need to make the right decisions about your Web site.

shopPBS

from the comfort of your own computer chair

http://www.pbs.org/shop

Now your favorite PBS videos and products are just a mouse click away with shopPBS.

At this special cyber shop you'll find a video collection with more than 200 titles, a bookshelf that includes the acclaimed book *NetLearning: How Teachers Use the Internet* and other fun items like the lovable Wishbone doll. Best of all, ordering is done online with secure credit card transactions!

For a fun-filled shopping adventure, make your next online stop shopPBS.

http://www.pbs.org/shop

PBS ONLINE® (http://www.pbs.org) is the premier choice for unique and compelling interactive content developed specifically for the Internet.

IF PBS DOESN'T DO IT, WHO WILL? http://www.pbs.org/shop

How to stay in touch with O'Reilly

1. Visit Our Award-Winning Web Site
http://www.ora.com/

★ "Top 100 Sites on the Web" —*PC Magazine*
★ "Top 5% Web sites" —*Point Communications*
★ "3-Star site" —*The McKinley Group*

Our web site contains a library of comprehensive product information (including book excerpts and tables of contents), downloadable software, background articles, interviews with technology leaders, links to relevant sites, book cover art, and more. File us in your Bookmarks or Hotlist!

2. Join Our Two Email Mailing Lists
#1 New Product Releases
To receive automatic email with brief descriptions of all new O'Reilly products as they are released, send email to:
listproc@online.ora.com
Put the following information in the first line of your message (*not* in the Subject field):
subscribe ora-news "Your Name"of "Your Organization" (for example: subscribe ora-news Kris Webber of Fine Enterprises)

#2 O'Reilly Events:
If you'd also like us to send information about trade show events, special promotions, and other O'Reilly events, send email to: **listproc@online.ora.com**
Put the following information in the first line of your message (*not* in the Subject field):
subscribe ora-events "Your Name" of "Your Organization"

3. Get Examples from Our Books via FTP
There are two ways to access an archive of example files from our books:

#1 Regular FTP
• ftp to:
ftp.ora.com
(login: anonymous
password: your email address)
• Point your web browser to:
ftp://ftp.ora.com/

#2 FTPMAIL
• Send an email message to:
ftpmail@online.ora.com
(Write "help" in the message body)

4. Visit Our Gopher Site
• Connect your gopher to
gopher.ora.com

• Point your web browser to:
gopher://gopher.ora.com/

• Telnet to:
gopher.ora.com
login: gopher

5. Contact Us via Email
order@ora.com
To place a book or software order online. Good for North American and international customers.

subscriptions@ora.com
To place an order for any of our newsletters or periodicals.

books@ora.com
General questions about any of our books.

software@ora.com
For general questions and product information about our software. Check out O'Reilly Software Online at **http://software.ora.com/** for software and technical support information. Registered O'Reilly software users send your questions to: **website-support@ora.com**

cs@ora.com
For answers to problems regarding your order or our products.

booktech@ora.com
For book content technical questions or corrections.

proposals@ora.com
To submit new book or software proposals to our editors and product managers.

international@ora.com
For information about our international distributors or translation queries. For a list of our distributors outside of North America check out:
http://www.ora.com/www/order/country.html

O'Reilly & Associates, Inc.
101 Morris Street, Sebastopol, CA 95472 USA
TEL 707-829-0515 or 800-998-9938
(6 a.m. to 5 p.m. pst)
FAX 707-829-0104

O'REILLY™

Titles from O'Reilly

Please note that upcoming titles are displayed in italic.

WEB PROGRAMMING

Apache: The Definitive Guide
Building Your Own Website
CGI Programming for the World Wide Web
Designing for the Web
HTML: The Definitive Guide
JavaScript: The Definitive Guide, 2nd Ed.
Learning Perl
Programming Perl, 2nd Ed.
Mastering Regular Expressions
WebMaster in a Nutshell
Web Security & Commerce
Web Client Programming with Perl
World Wide Web Journal

USING THE INTERNET

Smileys
The Future Does Not Compute
The Whole Internet User's Guide & Catalog
The Whole Internet for Win 95
Using Email Effectively
Bandits on the Information Superhighway

JAVA SERIES

Exploring Java
Java AWT Reference
Java Fundamental Classes Reference
Java in a Nutshell
Java Language Reference
Java Network Programming
Java Threads
Java Virtual Machine

SOFTWARE

WebSite™ 1.1
WebSite Professional™
Building Your Own Web Conferences
WebBoard™
PolyForm™
Statisphere™

SONGLINE GUIDES

NetActivism
Net Law
NetLearning
Net Lessons
NetResearch
NetSuccess for Realtors
NetTravel

SYSTEM ADMINISTRATION

Building Internet Firewalls
Computer Crime: A Crimefighter's Handbook
Computer Security Basics
DNS and BIND, 2nd Ed.
Essential System Administration, 2nd Ed.
Getting Connected: The Internet at 56K and Up
Internet Server Administration with Windows NT
Linux Network Administrator's Guide
Managing Internet Information Services
Managing NFS and NIS
Networking Personal Computers with TCP/IP
Practical UNIX & Internet Security. 2nd Ed.
PGP: Pretty Good Privacy
sendmail, 2nd Ed.
sendmail Desktop Reference
System Performance Tuning
TCP/IP Network Administration
termcap & terminfo
Using & Managing UUCP
Volume 8: X Window System Administrator's Guide
Web Security & Commerce

UNIX

Exploring Expect
Learning VBScript
Learning GNU Emacs, 2nd Ed.
Learning the bash Shell
Learning the Korn Shell
Learning the UNIX Operating System
Learning the vi Editor
Linux in a Nutshell
Making TeX Work
Linux Multimedia Guide
Running Linux, 2nd Ed.
SCO UNIX in a Nutshell
sed & awk, 2nd Edition
Tcl/Tk Tools
UNIX in a Nutshell: System V Edition
UNIX Power Tools
Using csh & tsch
When You Can't Find Your UNIX System Administrator
Writing GNU Emacs Extensions

WEB REVIEW STUDIO SERIES

Gif Animation Studio
Shockwave Studio

WINDOWS

Dictionary of PC Hardware and Data Communications Terms
Inside the Windows 95 Registry
Inside the Windows 95 File System
Win95 & WinNT Annoyances
Windows NT File System Internals
Windows NT in a Nutshell

PROGRAMMING

Advanced Oracle PL/SQL Programming
Applying RCS and SCCS
C++: The Core Language
Checking C Programs with lint
DCE Security Programming
Distributing Applications Across DCE & Windows NT
Encyclopedia of Graphics File Formats, 2nd Ed.
Guide to Writing DCE Applications
lex & yacc
Managing Projects with make
Mastering Oracle Power Objects
Oracle Design: The Definitive Guide
Oracle Performance Tuning, 2nd Ed.
Oracle PL/SQL Programming
Porting UNIX Software
POSIX Programmer's Guide
POSIX.4: Programming for the Real World
Power Programming with RPC
Practical C Programming
Practical C++ Programming
Programming Python
Programming with curses
Programming with GNU Software
Pthreads Programming
Software Portability with imake, 2nd Ed.
Understanding DCE
Understanding Japanese Information Processing
UNIX Systems Programming for SVR4

BERKELEY 4.4 SOFTWARE DISTRIBUTION

4.4BSD System Manager's Manual
4.4BSD User's Reference Manual
4.4BSD User's Supplementary Documents
4.4BSD Programmer's Reference Manual
4.4BSD Programmer's Supplementary Documents
X Programming
Vol. 0: X Protocol Reference Manual
Vol. 1: Xlib Programming Manual
Vol. 2: Xlib Reference Manual
Vol. 3M: X Window System User's Guide, Motif Edition
Vol. 4M: X Toolkit Intrinsics Programming Manual, Motif Edition
Vol. 5: X Toolkit Intrinsics Reference Manual
Vol. 6A: Motif Programming Manual
Vol. 6B: Motif Reference Manual
Vol. 6C: Motif Tools
Vol. 8 : X Window System Administrator's Guide
Programmer's Supplement for Release 6
X User Tools
The X Window System in a Nutshell

CAREER & BUSINESS

Building a Successful Software Business
The Computer User's Survival Guide
Love Your Job!
Electronic Publishing on CD-ROM

TRAVEL

Travelers' Tales: Brazil
Travelers' Tales: Food
Travelers' Tales: France
Travelers' Tales: Gutsy Women
Travelers' Tales: India
Travelers' Tales: Mexico
Travelers' Tales: Paris
Travelers' Tales: San Francisco
Travelers' Tales: Spain
Travelers' Tales: Thailand
Travelers' Tales: A Woman's World

O'REILLY™

TO ORDER: **800-998-9938** • **order@ora.com** • **http://www.ora.com/**
OUR PRODUCTS ARE AVAILABLE AT A BOOKSTORE OR SOFTWARE STORE NEAR YOU.

International Distributors

Europe, Middle East and Northern Africa (except
France, Germany, Switzerland, & Austria)

INQUIRIES
International Thomson Publishing Europe
Berkshire House
168-173 High Holborn
London WC1V 7AA, United Kingdom
Telephone: 44-171-497-1422
Fax: 44-171-497-1426
Email: itpint@itps.co.uk

ORDERS
International Thomson Publishing Services, Ltd.
Cheriton House, North Way
Andover, Hampshire SP10 5BE, United Kingdom
Telephone: 44-264-342-832
  (UK orders)
Telephone: 44-264-342-806
  (outside UK)
Fax: 44-264-364418 (UK orders)
Fax: 44-264-342761 (outside UK)
UK & Eire orders: itpuk@itps.co.uk
International orders: itpint@itps.co.uk

France
Editions Eyrolles
61 Bd Saint-Germain
75240 Paris Cedex 05
France
Telephone: 33 1 44 41 46 16
Fax: 33 1 44 41 11 44

Australia
WoodsLane Pty. Ltd.
7/5 Vuko Place, Warriewood NSW 2102
P.O. Box 935, Mona Vale NSW 2103
Australia
Telephone: 61-2-9970-5111
Fax: 61-2-9970-5002
Email: info@woodslane.com.au

Germany, Switzerland, and Austria
INQUIRIES
O'Reilly Verlag
Balthasarstr. 81
D-50670 Köln
Germany
Telephone: 49 221 97 31 60 0
Fax: 49 221 97 31 60 8
Email: anfragen@oreilly.de

ORDERS
International Thomson Publishing
Königswinterer Straße 418
53227 Bonn, Germany
Telephone: 49-228-97024 0
Fax: 49-228-441342
Email: order@oreilly.de

Asia (except Japan & India)
INQUIRIES
International Thomson Publishing Asia
60 Albert Street #15-01
Albert Complex
Singapore 189969
Telephone: 65-336-6411
Fax: 65-336-7411

ORDERS
Telephone: 65-336-6411
Fax: 65-334-1617
thomson@signet.com.sg

New Zealand
WoodsLane New Zealand Ltd.
21 Cooks Street (P.O. Box 575)
Wanganui, New Zealand
Telephone: 64-6-347-6543
Fax: 64-6-345-4840
Email: info@woodslane.com.au

Japan
O'Reilly Japan, Inc.
Kiyoshige Building 2F
12-Banchi, Sanei-cho
Shinjuku-ku
Tokyo 160 Japan
Telephone: 81-3-3356-5227
Fax: 81-3-3356-5261
Email: kenji@ora.com

India
Computer Bookshop (India) PVT. LTD.
190 Dr. D.N. Road, Fort
Bombay 400 001
India
Telephone: 91-22-207-0989
Fax: 91-22-262-3551
Email: cbsbom@giasbm01.vsnl.net.in

The Americas
O'Reilly & Associates, Inc.
101 Morris Street
Sebastopol, CA 95472 U.S.A.
Telephone: 707-829-0515
Telephone: 800-998-9938 (U.S. & Canada)
Fax: 707-829-0104
Email: order@ora.com

Southern Africa
International Thomson Publishing Southern Africa
Building 18, Constantia Park
240 Old Pretoria Road
P.O. Box 2459
Halfway House, 1685 South Africa
Telephone: 27-11-805-4819
Fax: 27-11-805-3648

O'REILLY™

O'Reilly & Associates, Inc.
101 Morris Street
Sebastopol, CA 95472-9902
1-800-998-9938

Visit us online at:
http://www.ora.com/
orders@ora.com

O'REILLY WOULD LIKE TO HEAR FROM YOU

Which book did this card come from?

_____

Where did you buy this book?
❏ Bookstore ❏ Computer Store
❏ Direct from O'Reilly ❏ Class/seminar
❏ Bundled with hardware/software
❏ Other _____

What operating system do you use?
❏ UNIX ❏ Macintosh
❏ Windows NT ❏ PC(Windows/DOS)
❏ Other _____

What is your job description?
❏ System Administrator ❏ Programmer
❏ Network Administrator ❏ Educator/Teacher
❏ Web Developer
❏ Other _____

❏ Please send me O'Reilly's catalog, containing
a complete listing of O'Reilly books and
software.

Name _____ Company/Organization _____

Address _____

City _____ State _____ Zip/Postal Code _____ Country _____

Telephone _____ Internet or other email address (specify network) _____

Nineteenth century wood engraving
of a bear from the O'Reilly &
Associates Nutshell Handbook®
Using & Managing UUCP.

POST CARD

BUSINESS REPLY MAIL
FIRST CLASS MAIL   PERMIT NO. 80   SEBASTOPOL, CA

Postage will be paid by addressee

O'Reilly & Associates, Inc.
101 Morris Street
Sebastopol, CA 95472-9902